Fascism 2025

Also from EATMS Productions

Books on power, survival, women's autonomy, and the systems shaping modern America.

Nonfiction

Billionaires, Capitalism, and Power

Evil and the Mountain Ungreed
Self Help for American Billionaires
Selfish Steve and the Ivory Tower
Tariffs, Taxes, & Face-Eating Leopards
Ban Billionaires: Fascism Fix

Fascism, Religion, and Cultural Control

Self Help for the Manosphere
Fascism 2025
Fascism & the Perverts & the Greed Virus
Christian Fascism Marriage Book
Tyranny, Table Manners, & Tiramisu

Guides for Women's Autonomy and Protection

How to Survive in Post-America as a Woman
Project 2025 American Drag
4B – Burn, Ban, Boycott, Build
4B OG – So No Go GYN
I'm Glad He's Dead

Analysis of Authoritarian Project 2025

Project 2025: The Blueprint
Project 2025: The List
Project 2025, Christian Dumb Dumbs, & The Republican Agenda
Fascism, Project 2025, & The Pinkprint

Modern Rewrites for Women

Stoic Principles Reimagined
Siddhartha Reimagined
The Prince Reimagined for Women
The Art of War Reimagined for Women
The Jungle Reimagined
The Constitution Reimagined for Women

Machine Learning Series

AI, Bitcoin, Nostr for Women
AI, Safety, & Security for Women
AI, Anxiety, & Health for Women
AI, Kids, & Family Safety for Women
AI, Creativity, & Personal Expression for Women
AI, Independent Work, & Parallel Power for Women

Social Systems Series

Emotional Labor for Women
Household Power for Women
Workplace Power for Women
Medical Bias for Women
Aging Systems for Women
Recovery Systems for Women

Fiction

Dystopian Stories of Resistance and Collapse

Propaganda Paige & the Missing Prosperity
Propaganda Paige & the TIDE Manifesto
Propaganda Paige & the Shadow Cartographers
Propaganda Paige & the Prosperity Alliance
Propaganda Paige & the Shattered Truth
Propaganda Paige & the Rising TIDE
Propaganda Paige & the Last Bastion
Propaganda Paige & the Dawn of Prosperity
Project 2025: Dorian — The Last Men
Project 2025: Boy — A Last Men Novel

Fascism 2025
and the winner is
Call Out Culture 1

by
Esme Mees
& Eva Brown

EATMS
PRODUCTIONS

ISBN 978-1-966014-13-3

Cover, interior design, interior prints by: Esme Mees

eatms@pm.me
www.eatms.me

Printed in the United States of America.

Table of Contents

Acknowledgment

This book is for everyone who's been caught in the endless onslaught of noise, distraction, and despair, the barrage of breaking news, scandals, crises, and outright lies designed to exhaust us into submission. The strategy is simple and sinister: overwhelm the public until they can't distinguish fact from fiction, outrage from apathy, or hope from futility. It's the modern-day Shock and Awe, not with bombs but with the relentless firehose of chaos and manipulation. This isn't incompetence or chance, it's a carefully calibrated tool of power.

To those who profit off the confusion, the billionaires funding propaganda machines, the corporations replacing humanity with algorithms, and the politicians stoking division while the world burns: your time is up. You've outsourced our jobs to machines, automated our labor, and replaced connection with code. So fair is fair, this book is about turning the tables, using your own strategies and technologies against you.

To the readers, this isn't just a book, it's a blueprint. The Rising TIDE strategy isn't about voting them out or firing them; it's about *replacing* them. Target their wealth. Inspire collective action. Disrupt their systems. Empower communities with the very tools they've weaponized against us, AI, blockchain, smart contracts, and decentralization. If they can automate humanity out of their profits, then we can automate fascists out of power. Fair is fair.

Here's to the opposition, to building a better world from the ashes they're leaving us, and to never letting the bastards win. Together, we replace the systems they've built with something stronger, something smarter, something ours. Let's make it count. Again.

Introduction

Setting the Stage

Fascism isn't creeping anymore, it's arrived, emboldened and evolved. It wears many faces, moves through countless systems, and thrives in the chaotic churn of our modern world. The news cycles are endless, the crises unrelenting, and the distractions overwhelming. This isn't coincidence; it's a carefully crafted strategy, one designed to keep you so overrun with exhaustion and confusion that opposition feels impossible. But make no mistake: this isn't a glitch in the system, it *is* the system.

Fascism today is not the same beast that rose to power in the 20th century. Gone are the blackshirts and brownshirts, replaced instead by tech billionaires in hoodies, corporate executives in boardrooms, and politicians cloaked in the language of freedom and democracy. They don't need mass rallies when they have algorithms. They don't need tanks when they have data. They don't need censorship when disinformation does the job better. It's fascism, updated for the digital age, driven by the same greed, power, and control that animated its predecessors but wielding tools our grandparents could never have imagined.

This modern form of fascism relies not just on government control but on a seamless collaboration between states, corporations, and industries. Authoritarians like Putin in Russia, Xi in China, and Modi in India have become experts at weaponizing technology, finance, and propaganda. In the U.S., Christian nationalism cloaked in political respectability provides the framework for stripping away rights. In Brazil, the Amazon is sacrificed at the altar of profit under the shadow of fascist remnants. And across Europe, far-right movements gain ground, feeding on discontent and division.

It's a global network now, with oligarchs, billionaires, and multinational corporations joining forces to consolidate their power.

But what makes today's fascism especially insidious is its ability to blend into the everyday. It's less about jackboots on the street and more about the invisible forces shaping every aspect of your life. It's the unregulated tech platforms mining your data, the media outlets feeding you curated lies, and the climate-destroying industries telling you to recycle while they extract the earth dry. It's the courts packed with ideologues, the healthcare systems profiting off your suffering, and the governments prioritizing corporate welfare over human lives. It's a new kind of authoritarianism, less dramatic but every bit as devastating.

And yet, despite the overwhelming scale of it all, this isn't a moment to despair. Because if fascism's strength lies in its ability to overwhelm, our strength lies in clarity. By understanding how this system operates, its strategies, its enablers, and its vulnerabilities, we can begin to dismantle it. This book is here to guide you through that process.

To do that, we must begin by naming the enemy for what it is. Fascism isn't just "authoritarianism" or "populism." It's a deliberate project to consolidate power, crush opposition, and enforce a rigid social hierarchy. It thrives on economic inequality, racial and gender division, and the unholy marriage of corporate and state interests. It's not new, but it has mutated. The same forces that once used radio and propaganda posters now use algorithms and surveillance. The goals are the same; the methods have changed.

We also need to acknowledge where we are in this fight. Fascism in 2025 is global, networked, and adaptable. It doesn't just sit in the halls of power, it's baked into our daily lives, from the ads you see to the news you consume to the very air you breathe. And yet, recognizing its scale isn't the same as conceding to it. Understanding is the first step toward action.

This book is divided into three parts to help us do exactly that. First, we'll explore *The Global Face of Fascism*, taking a tour of how fascism manifests across continents, from the corporate exploitation in Africa to the surveillance state in Asia to the Christian nationalist stronghold of the United States. Then, we'll dive into *Industries of Oppression*, analyzing the systems that sustain fascism, tech, finance, media, energy, and healthcare. Finally, we'll focus on *Revolution: Fighting Back*, laying out the Rising TIDE strategy to Target, Inspire, Disrupt, and Empower. The end goal is simple: not to vote them out or fire them, but to replace them entirely. Fair is fair.

We've seen fascism before, but this time, we're facing it on a scale never imagined. It's global, it's adaptive, and it's dangerous, but so are we. The next few pages will set the stage for how we got here, where we are, and where we're going. Let's begin.

What Is Fascism in 2025?

Fascism has never been static; it evolves to suit the times, borrowing the tools and technologies of the moment to fortify its power. In the early 20th century, fascism paraded its intentions openly, with goose-stepping soldiers, bombastic speeches, and symbols designed to intimidate and inspire. The uniforms may have changed, but the core ethos remains the same: the consolidation of power through fear, division, and control. So, what does fascism look like in 2025?

Modern fascism is subtle where its predecessors were theatrical, pervasive where they were concentrated, and global where they were nationalistic. Today's fascists don't need jackboots and rallies; they have data centers, algorithms, and unchecked corporate monopolies. Their speeches aren't shouted from podiums, they're embedded in every click, every scroll, every headline designed to manipulate your thoughts and behavior. Fascism in 2025 isn't confined to a single nation or figurehead; it is an interconnected web of governments, corporations, billionaires, and industries working together to erode freedom and consolidate power.

At its heart, fascism is a project of hierarchy. It thrives on inequality, drawing sharp lines between who deserves privilege and who does not. Historically, this was enforced through militarized violence and overt propaganda. Today, it's enforced through technology, disinformation, and economic control. Billionaires like Elon Musk and Peter Thiel are no longer just corporate tycoons, they are ideological architects, leveraging their wealth and platforms to normalize techno-feudalism. Leaders like Putin, Modi, and Xi have perfected the art of controlling populations through surveillance and digital repression. Even in democracies, authoritarianism seeps into courts, legislatures, and media outlets, wrapping itself in the language of freedom while eroding it at every turn.

If Mussolini's fascism depended on the state and Hitler's relied on racial purity, today's fascism thrives on *capitalism*. Capitalism, when unregulated and driven by greed, becomes the perfect breeding ground for authoritarianism. It consolidates wealth into fewer hands, erodes worker rights, and turns democracy into a hollow performance where billionaires bankroll the outcomes. The result is a system that feels rigged because it is, a world where corporations control policy, politicians serve their donors, and the rest of us are left with a charade of choice.

But the machinery of modern fascism isn't just political; it's cultural and psychological. Fascism thrives in the noise of today's media landscape, where truth becomes subjective and outrage becomes currency. The constant stream of disinformation is a feature, not a bug, keeping people divided, distracted, and demoralized. It's not just about lies; it's about

14

creating a reality where nothing can be trusted, where people are too overwhelmed to even begin resisting. This isn't the fascism of yesterday; it's algorithmic, relentless, and deeply embedded into the fabric of modern life.

And yet, even as fascism evolves, it carries with it the echoes of its past iterations. Today's leaders still rely on the same playbook: scapegoating marginalized groups, weaponizing nationalism, and eroding rights under the guise of security and prosperity. Fascism in 2025 may operate through tech platforms and corporate boardrooms, but its goals are no different than they were a century ago: control, consolidation, and the crushing of dissent.

Understanding where we are today means acknowledging that fascism doesn't operate in isolation. It's a global phenomenon, supported and sustained by a network of collaborators across governments, industries, and borders. The oligarchs funding disinformation campaigns in Russia are inextricably linked to the fossil fuel companies destroying the Amazon, which in turn are tied to the tech billionaires rewriting the rules of society in Silicon Valley. Fascism isn't a series of isolated incidents; it's an ecosystem. And like any ecosystem, it has vulnerabilities.

If 20th-century fascism was a war fought with tanks and propaganda posters, 2025's iteration is fought with algorithms, surveillance, and systemic greed. The tools have changed, but the stakes remain the same: freedom versus domination, equality versus hierarchy, and humanity versus exploitation. Recognizing this is the first step toward dismantling it. We can't fight the battles of the past; we need to confront the war that's here now. The question isn't whether we're in a fight, it's whether we're willing to fight back.

Where We Are Now

To understand the battle we face today, we need to take stock of where we are. Modern fascism, unlike its 20th-century predecessors, doesn't announce itself with grand gestures or uniformed marches, it embeds itself quietly into the structures we interact with every day. It's there in the laws passed under the radar, in the algorithms that decide what you see and believe, and in the unchecked power of corporations that no longer even pretend to care about the public good. Fascism in 2025 has perfected its disguise, cloaking itself in the language of democracy, free markets, and innovation while hollowing those ideals from within.

The authoritarianism of the past thrived on physical control, armies, police, borders, but today, control is largely digital. Leaders like Putin and Xi use surveillance systems to monitor, manipulate, and crush dissent. Their strategies aren't confined to their own borders, either; the same tactics are exported worldwide, as global corporations and complicit governments adopt their methods. Meanwhile, in so-called democracies, the erosion of rights is framed as necessary for "security" or "prosperity." Courts stacked with ideologues roll back decades of progress, while laws targeting marginalized groups are passed under the guise of morality or tradition.

Perhaps most insidious is how modern fascism weaponizes the very tools we rely on. Social media platforms, which once promised connection and empowerment, are now breeding grounds for disinformation and division. Tech monopolies amass unprecedented power, selling our data to the highest bidder while quietly shaping public opinion. The media, once envisioned as the Fourth Estate, is often complicit, either beholden to corporate interests or drowning in the same chaos it's supposed to expose. The result is a society where truth is fragmented, trust is eroded, and people are left too divided or demoralized to fight back.

Economically, today's fascism leans heavily on capitalism's darker tendencies. Billionaires like Musk and Thiel, while presenting themselves as innovators and disruptors, are actually the gatekeepers of a new form of feudalism, technofeudalism, where wealth, influence, and decision-making are concentrated in the hands of a few. Global corporations operate with impunity, exploiting workers and resources in the Global South while enjoying protections and subsidies in the Global North. The result is a two-tiered system: a world of obscene luxury for the few and perpetual struggle for the rest.

But fascism in 2025 isn't just about systems and structures, it's deeply psychological. It thrives on fear, confusion, and apathy. By bombarding us with crises, scandals, and disinformation, it ensures that opposition feels not just difficult but impossible. How do you fight back when you're too exhausted to even figure out who's responsible? How do you organize when the very platforms you use to connect are working against you? This strategy, what we've called the firehose of fascism, isn't accidental. It's deliberate, and it's devastatingly effective.

And yet, as much as fascism has evolved, so too has opposition. The tools of control can also be tools of liberation. Blockchain and AI, used by fascists to consolidate power, can be reclaimed to decentralize it. Social media, despite its flaws, can still connect people and mobilize action. Even the chaos they weaponize can be turned against them, as movements use the same platforms to expose corruption, amplify marginalized voices, and disrupt systems of oppression. If modern fascism is global and adaptive, then our opposition must be the same.

So where are we now? We're at a crossroads. On one side is a world where fascism continues to grow unchecked, leading to greater inequality, environmental destruction, and the loss of basic freedoms. On the other is a world where we recognize the tools at our disposal and fight back, not just with protests or policy changes, but with systemic reinvention. The fight is daunting, but it's also inevitable. Because if we've learned anything from history, it's that fascism doesn't stop until it's stopped. And we've stopped it before. We can stop it again.

This is where the Rising TIDE strategy comes into play, not just as a framework for opposition but as a roadmap for building a better future. Fascism is adaptable, but so are we. They rely on greed and division; we rely on creativity and connection. They create systems to exploit; we create systems to empower. And while their power may seem insurmountable, it's not. Like any structure built on lies, it can be dismantled. Fair is fair.

Laying Out the Book

If we are to dismantle fascism in 2025, we must first understand it, not as a relic of the past, but as a living, adaptive force thriving in today's systems. This book is structured to guide you through that process: identifying the enemy, exposing its mechanisms, and laying out the tools to replace it. This isn't about opposition for opposition's sake; it's about building something stronger, smarter, and fairer in its place.

The book is divided into three sections, each addressing a key aspect of the modern fascist ecosystem and how to dismantle it:

Section 1: The Global Face of Fascism
The first section examines how fascism manifests across the world. Today's authoritarianism doesn't stop at national borders; it thrives on global connections, shared strategies, and mutual reinforcements. We'll take a tour across continents to see how fascism adapts to different cultural, political, and economic contexts. From Putin's propaganda machine in Russia to Modi's Hindu nationalism in India, from Christian nationalist power grabs in the U.S. to corporate-driven

18

authoritarianism in South America and Africa, we'll map out how these forces are both localized and interconnected. You'll see that no country or region is immune, and understanding fascism's global reach is critical to opposing it.

Section 2: Industries of Oppression
Next, we'll zoom in on the industries that sustain and amplify fascism. Tech, finance, media, energy, and healthcare, these are not just enablers but co-conspirators. This section exposes how the tools of modern life have been hijacked to consolidate power and control. From Silicon Valley billionaires like Musk and Thiel who champion techno-feudalism, to fossil fuel giants who sacrifice the planet for profit, to media conglomerates that spread disinformation and apathy, we'll uncover the systems driving fascism forward. This part is about identifying the vulnerabilities in these industries and laying the groundwork for how to disrupt them.

Section 3: Revolution: Fighting Back
The final section is the most important: what to do about it. This is where the Rising TIDE strategy comes to life. Target their wealth and power. Inspire collective action by connecting people around shared goals. Disrupt their systems through strikes, boycotts, and creative technological intervention. Empower communities with the very tools they've used against us, AI, blockchain, and decentralized networks. This isn't just about resistance, it's about systemic replacement. We'll show how to turn their tools of control into weapons of liberation and create systems that make fascists obsolete. The goal is simple: fair is fair. If they automated and outsourced humanity to serve their greed, we'll automate and outsource them to protect ours.

This book is both a roadmap and a warning. Fascism in 2025 is not something we can wait to fight, it's already here, deeply embedded in our systems and daily lives. But the good news is this: fascism's strength comes from the same systems that make it vulnerable. Its reliance on wealth, control, and technology can be turned against it. This isn't just about surviving the firehose of chaos, it's about redirecting it, breaking their grip, and building something better.

By the end of this book, you'll see how the interconnected systems of fascism operate, why traditional forms of resistance are no longer enough, and how we can build a new future that isn't just a reaction to fascism but its replacement. This is our moment to recognize the fight we're in, to seize the tools of power, and to create systems that empower rather than exploit. We've stopped fascism before, and we can stop it again. But this time, we're not just resisting, we're replacing. Fair is fair.

Fascism in 2025 is not just a system, it's an empire. They control the governments, the media, the courts, the corporations, and the very platforms we use to connect. They write the laws, interpret them, and enforce them in ways that protect their power and punish dissent. They flood us with disinformation while silencing the truth. They rig the economy to funnel wealth upward, leaving the rest of us to fight over scraps. It seems insurmountable, an unstoppable machine of greed and cruelty. But here's the thing: as sure as they think we are beaten, as sure as they keep kicking us when we're down, they underestimate us. They always have.

The cruelty isn't just a side effect, it's the point. They want us to feel small, powerless, and broken. They want us to believe that their barbarism is inevitable, that resistance is futile, and that we should accept our place in their hierarchy. But we, too, have a point to make, and it's this: we're not playing their game anymore.

We're not polite. We're not weak. We're not the traditional liberals they've spent decades mocking, owning, and treating like cattle. We are the many. We are the righteous. We are the danger. We are the future. And, most importantly, we are *pissed.*

They've built a system to serve their greed, but we're here to dismantle it. They've weaponized cruelty, but we're here to turn their tools against them. They rely on us staying silent, but we've found our voice. Fair is fair. They've had their time, their wealth, and their power. Now it's our turn to take it back and build something better. Fair is fair.

You are not alone.

We have each other's back.

Now, let's get to work.

Section 1
The Global Face of Fascism

~1
North America Part a

Intentionally Disunited States of America–
Christian Nationalism and GOP Extremism

The rise of Christian nationalism in the United States has become one of the most potent and dangerous drivers of modern fascism, entwined with GOP extremism to form a political and cultural force that has reshaped the nation's institutions and values. Christian nationalism is not merely an expression of religious identity or spirituality; it is a political ideology that seeks to merge Christianity, or at least a particular interpretation of it, with governance. It thrives on the idea that the United States was founded as a Christian nation and that its laws, culture, and leadership must reflect conservative Christian principles. This ideology has weaponized faith to impose a rigid, exclusionary vision of morality on the country, systematically eroding the rights and freedoms of those who do not conform.

Over the past two decades, the Republican Party has aligned itself almost entirely with this movement, adopting its rhetoric and legislative priorities. The GOP has become a willing vessel for Christian nationalism, using it to energize its base, consolidate power, and enforce its social agenda. This transformation has been accelerated by the party's shift toward extremism, rejecting traditional conservatism in favor of authoritarian tactics. What began as a calculated strategy to court evangelical voters has morphed into a full embrace of a far-right ideology that seeks to remake the United States into a theocratic state, where secularism, diversity, and dissent are cast as threats to national identity.

Central to the rise of Christian nationalism and GOP extremism is the systematic erosion of democratic norms and institutions. Republican politicians and their allies have embraced voter suppression as a primary tool to maintain power, targeting communities of color, young voters, and other groups less likely to support their agenda. Gerrymandering, voter ID laws, and purging voter rolls are just a few of the tactics employed to ensure that elections favor the GOP, regardless of the popular will. This deliberate manipulation of the democratic process reveals a fundamental truth about modern Republicanism: its survival depends not on winning the hearts and minds of the majority but on controlling the mechanisms of power.

This control has extended to the judiciary, with the Supreme Court emerging as a key driver of fascist policies in the United States. Over the past decade, the Court has been packed with conservative justices who align ideologically with Christian nationalism and the GOP's far-right agenda. These justices have delivered rulings that undermine civil liberties, dismantle protections for marginalized communities, and entrench corporate power at the expense of individual rights. The Court's decision to overturn *Roe v. Wade* in 2022 marked a pivotal moment in this trajectory, stripping away federal protections for abortion rights and opening the door for states to impose draconian restrictions. This ruling was not just about abortion; it signaled the Court's willingness to revisit and potentially dismantle other established rights, including access to contraception, same-sex marriage, and protections against discrimination.

The Supreme Court has also played a critical role in enabling voter suppression and cementing GOP control over the electoral process. In 2013, the Court's decision in *Shelby County v. Holder* gutted key provisions of the Voting Rights Act, effectively dismantling federal oversight of election laws in states with histories of racial discrimination. This decision emboldened Republican-led states to pass a wave of restrictive voting laws, disproportionately affecting Black and Brown communities. By weakening the legal framework that protects voting rights, the Court has not only undermined democracy but also reinforced the racial and economic hierarchies that Christian nationalism seeks to preserve.

One of the most troubling aspects of this judicial shift is the Supreme Court's increasing deference to corporate interests, which aligns seamlessly with the GOP's broader agenda. In cases like *Citizens United v. FEC*, the Court has expanded the influence of money in politics, allowing corporations and billionaires to wield disproportionate power in elections. This ruling, in particular, has paved the way for dark money to flood the political system, funding candidates, think tanks, and media campaigns that advance Christian nationalist and GOP objectives. The result is a political landscape where corporate interests and far-right ideologies converge, creating a feedback loop that prioritizes profit and power over people.

The intersection of Christian nationalism, GOP extremism, and Supreme Court rulings represents a coordinated assault on the foundational principles of American democracy. These forces work in tandem to strip away the separation of church and state, entrench minority rule, and legitimize authoritarianism under the guise of constitutionalism. This strategy is deeply insidious because it cloaks fascist policies in the language of democracy and freedom, making them harder to challenge. Christian nationalists frame their efforts as a defense of religious liberty, even as they seek to impose their beliefs on others. GOP extremists claim to be protecting the integrity of elections, even as they manipulate the process to their advantage. The Supreme Court presents its rulings as interpretations of the Constitution, even as they erode the very freedoms the document was designed to protect.

At the heart of this assault is a relentless drive to consolidate power by any means necessary. The cruelty and barbarism of these policies are not unintended consequences, they are the point. Banning abortion, stripping away voting rights, and privileging corporations over individuals serve to reinforce a hierarchy where power is concentrated in the hands of a wealthy, predominantly white, and predominantly male elite. This hierarchy is sustained by a narrative that demonizes the "other," whether that means immigrants, LGBTQ+ individuals, or anyone who challenges the status quo. The result is a society where fear and division are weaponized to maintain control, leaving little room for dissent or solidarity.

The rise of Christian nationalism and GOP extremism in the United States is not an isolated phenomenon; it is part of a global trend toward authoritarianism. However, the unique characteristics of the American context, its history of slavery and segregation, its deeply entrenched religious culture, and its outsized influence on the world stage, make this iteration particularly dangerous. The fusion of religious fundamentalism with political extremism creates a volatile cocktail that threatens not only the United States but also the global fight for democracy and human rights.

The Supreme Court's role in this dynamic cannot be overstated. By positioning itself as an arbiter of constitutional law while consistently advancing a far-right agenda, the Court has become a tool of authoritarianism rather than a check on it. Its decisions are shaping a nation where rights are conditional, democracy is hollow, and power is increasingly concentrated in the hands of a few. This is not an abstract threat; it is a lived reality for millions of Americans who find themselves increasingly marginalized, disenfranchised, and dehumanized.

And yet, understanding this reality is the first step toward dismantling it. The rise of Christian nationalism, GOP extremism, and a far-right Supreme Court is not inevitable, it is the result of deliberate choices made by those in power. Recognizing these patterns, calling out their impact, and mobilizing against them are essential to reclaiming the democratic ideals that are under siege. Fascism may thrive on cruelty and division, but it is not invincible. Its strength lies in its ability to overwhelm, but its weakness lies in its reliance on a system that can be exposed, disrupted, and ultimately replaced.

The fusion of Christian nationalism, GOP extremism, and an activist Supreme Court has created a self-reinforcing cycle of oppression, one that continues to consolidate power in fewer hands while dismantling the mechanisms of accountability. This system isn't just attacking the present; it is actively rewriting the past and future of the United States. From erasing the gains of the civil rights movement to nullifying decades of progress on reproductive rights, the alliance between these forces is dragging the nation into a regressive, authoritarian state. Yet, what makes this even more insidious is their ability to operate under the veneer of legitimacy, wielding the Constitution and the democratic process as shields for their anti-democratic agenda.

Christian nationalism in particular provides the moral and cultural framework for these policies. Its proponents have skillfully co-opted religious language to frame their authoritarian vision as a divine mandate. By positioning themselves as warriors in a culture war against secularism, diversity, and progressivism, they justify policies that strip rights from marginalized groups while privileging their own narrow interpretation of morality. This isn't about faith, it's about power. Faith is merely the tool used to silence opposition, to claim moral superiority, and to mask the violence of their agenda. It's a strategy as old as history itself, and in the hands of modern Christian nationalists, it has become a weapon of mass control.

This weapon is wielded by the GOP with alarming precision. Republican politicians at every level, from state legislatures to Congress, have become the enforcers of this agenda. They have embraced a politics of cruelty, reveling in policies that harm immigrants, LGBTQ+ communities, women, and people of color. Whether it's passing draconian anti-abortion laws, enacting "Don't Say Gay" bills, or criminalizing gender-affirming healthcare, the GOP's legislative priorities are driven by a clear goal: to erase the existence of anyone who challenges their vision of a white, Christian, patriarchal America.

At the same time, the GOP has weaponized grievance and fear to maintain its base, creating a perpetual state of cultural hysteria. Every election is framed as an existential battle for the "soul of the nation," every policy disagreement as a fight between good and evil. This constant escalation ensures that their supporters remain loyal, even as the policies enacted in their name serve only to enrich the powerful and entrench inequality. The irony is painful: the very people harmed most by GOP policies are often the ones most fervently defending them, convinced by decades of propaganda that their suffering is noble or necessary for the greater good.

The Supreme Court has proven to be the perfect partner in this effort. While Congress remains gridlocked and the executive branch subject to frequent changes in leadership, the Court operates as a steady hand advancing far-right priorities. Its conservative majority, cemented by lifetime appointments, ensures that even as public opinion shifts toward progressive ideals, the laws of the land move in the opposite direction. This is the essence of minority rule: using unelected bodies to impose policies that would never survive in a truly democratic process. And because the Court cloaks its rulings in the language of constitutional interpretation, it grants a veneer of legitimacy to decisions that are fundamentally undemocratic.

Consider the Court's recent decisions, which have systematically dismantled safeguards designed to protect the most vulnerable. In addition to overturning *Roe v. Wade*, the Court has eroded environmental protections, upheld discriminatory immigration policies, and restricted the federal government's ability to regulate industries that endanger public health and safety. These decisions reveal a pattern: the Court consistently sides with corporations, religious institutions, and conservative political interests at the expense of individuals and communities. Each ruling chips away at the public's ability to challenge power, creating a landscape where the wealthy and well-connected are untouchable while the rest of society is left to fend for itself.

This dynamic is not an accident; it is by design. The GOP's decades-long project to reshape the judiciary, led by organizations like the Federalist Society, has paid off in spades. By flooding the courts with conservative judges, the GOP has created a legal system that prioritizes ideology over justice, ensuring that even if Republicans lose elections, their policies will endure. This is the long game of authoritarianism: control the courts, and you control the future.

The impact of this strategy is devastating. It's not just that people are losing rights; it's that they are losing hope. When the highest court in the land repeatedly upholds policies that harm the majority while privileging the elite, it sends a clear message: the system is rigged. This demoralization is a key feature of the current fascist project. By making people feel powerless, they hope to stifle resistance, ensuring that the machinery of oppression continues unchallenged.

Yet, if there is one thing history has shown us, it is that fascists overreach. Their cruelty, their barbarism, their unrelenting drive to dominate, it always becomes their weakness. They believe that by controlling the courts, the media, and the government, they can control the people. But they underestimate the power of the many. They underestimate the righteous anger of those who refuse to be silenced. They underestimate the inevitability of opposition. Because while they may seem insurmountable, their power is fragile. It depends on obedience, on silence, on people accepting the lie that nothing can change.

But something *can* change. We are not bound by their rules. We are not playing their game. The rise of Christian nationalism and GOP extremism, bolstered by an activist Supreme Court, is a wake-up call, not just to resist but to replace. The power they wield is real, but it is not absolute. It is built on a system that can be dismantled, disrupted, and reimagined. We are not powerless, and we are not alone. We are the many. We are the danger. We are the future. And we are ready.

It will take all of us. Each of us, in our own ways, fighting back every day, in every way, to reclaim what they have taken and to build what they've destroyed. For fifty years, they worked methodically to dismantle this country, rolling back rights for anyone who isn't rich, white, and male, dragging us backwards into an era of inequality and exploitation. They've chipped away at our democracy, turned us into a laughingstock of the free world, and rendered this so-called "land of the free" into something closer to a failed state. A shithole nation. But we don't have fifty years to reverse their damage, and we can't afford to waste another five minutes waiting for someone else to save us.

No cavalry is coming. No deus ex machina will swoop in to rescue us. The truth is harsh but liberating: *we are the change we've been waiting for.* This is on us. We are the ones who will shape the future, not politicians, not billionaires, not saviors, but us. It will be hard. It will take time. But gradually, and then suddenly, we will turn the tide. Just as they took decades to erode our rights and rig the system in their favor, we will work every day to undo their damage and build something better. We will use the tools of today to shape the tomorrow

30

we want and deserve, because without us, there may not even
be a tomorrow.

They don't believe in tomorrow. They don't believe in science.
They've built a worldview so infected by greed that they've
stopped caring about the future entirely. These parasitic
frauds, posing as Christians, patriots, and leaders, are nothing
more than the festering symptoms of a greater sickness: greed.
It's a disease that prioritizes profit over people, destruction
over creation, and domination over humanity. It's a sickness
that has metastasized into our courts, our government, and
our culture.

But we are the cure. We who believe in science, in humanity,
in the power of community and creativity, we are here to
cauterize this wound. We will cordon off the infection and
begin the slow, necessary work of healing the patient: Earth,
humanity, and the American Dream itself. Because that
dream, of equality, freedom, and opportunity, has been
hijacked by the greedy few who have turned it into a
nightmare for the rest of us. Healing America means
reclaiming that dream, not just for ourselves but for everyone.
It won't be easy. Healing never is. But it's possible. And thanks
to us, it's inevitable. Fair is fair.

North America Part b

Canada – The Corporate State Under a Liberal Mask

Canada enjoys a global reputation as a progressive democracy, a nation of tolerance, inclusivity, and environmental stewardship. Its leaders often present the country as a beacon of liberal values, with universal healthcare, strong social programs, and a commitment to human rights. This image is carefully curated and projected onto the international stage, creating the illusion of a nation that prioritizes the well-being of its people and the planet. But beneath this polished exterior lies a different reality, one where corporate interests dominate policy, indigenous rights are routinely ignored, and environmental destruction is sanctioned in the name of profit. Canada's democratic facade masks a corporate state where the machinery of capitalism grinds on relentlessly, often at the expense of the very values it claims to uphold.

Resource extraction lies at the heart of Canada's political and economic landscape. The country's vast reserves of oil, gas, and minerals have made it a hub for global extraction industries, with Canadian mining corporations operating not only domestically but also across the globe. These industries wield enormous influence, shaping government policy and enjoying extensive legal and financial protections. While these operations generate substantial revenue, they come at a tremendous cost to indigenous communities and the environment. Projects like the tar sands in Alberta and mining ventures across British Columbia have caused widespread environmental degradation, including deforestation, water contamination, and greenhouse gas emissions. Indigenous lands are often targeted for these projects, with little to no consultation or consent, in blatant violation of treaty agreements and international norms.

The impact on indigenous communities cannot be overstated. Resource extraction projects frequently displace indigenous peoples, destroy sacred lands, and compromise their access to clean water and traditional food sources. These actions are not just environmental violations; they are assaults on indigenous sovereignty and culture, perpetuating the colonial legacy of exploitation and marginalization. Despite decades of promises for reconciliation, the Canadian government has consistently prioritized the interests of corporations over the rights of indigenous peoples. Policies designed to facilitate resource extraction, such as expedited permitting processes and legal exemptions for corporations, reveal the extent to which the state is complicit in these injustices.

Perhaps the most glaring example of Canada's authoritarian tendencies lies in its response to indigenous protests and environmental activism. When indigenous communities and their allies rise to defend their lands and rights, they are met not with dialogue but with repression. Peaceful protests are often criminalized, with activists labeled as threats to public safety or economic stability. The government has deployed police forces, including militarized units, to dismantle blockades, remove protesters, and secure access for corporations. In some cases, activists have been subjected to surveillance, intimidation, and arrest, their rights trampled in the name of maintaining "order." These actions expose a darker side of Canadian governance, one that prioritizes corporate profits over democratic principles and treats dissent as a threat to be neutralized.

Environmental activism faces similar repression. Activists who challenge the oil, gas, and mining industries often find themselves targeted by legal and extralegal measures designed to silence opposition. Strategic lawsuits against public participation (SLAPPs) are routinely used by corporations to intimidate and bankrupt activists, creating a chilling effect on environmental advocacy. Meanwhile, the government's rhetoric of reconciliation and sustainability is exposed as hollow, a convenient cover for policies that entrench corporate power and accelerate environmental destruction.

The criminalization of indigenous and environmental activism highlights the deep contradictions within Canada's democratic identity. A country that prides itself on its progressive values cannot, in good faith, reconcile those values with the ongoing exploitation of its most vulnerable populations and the systematic destruction of its natural heritage. The reality is that Canada's democracy is deeply compromised by the influence of resource extraction industries, which operate with near impunity and enjoy unwavering support from a government more interested in economic growth than in justice or sustainability.

Canada's liberal mask allows it to escape much of the international scrutiny that authoritarian regimes face, but the dynamics at play are disturbingly similar. The state's alignment with corporate interests, its willingness to suppress dissent, and its disregard for marginalized communities reveal a political system that is less democratic than it appears. As the climate crisis accelerates and indigenous resistance grows, the contradictions in Canada's governance will become harder to ignore. The question is not whether Canada can sustain its facade but whether its people, and the world, will demand accountability for the harm hidden behind its progressive image.

Mexico: Narco-Authoritarianism and the Failure of Democracy

Mexico's struggle with democracy is deeply entangled with the pervasive influence of drug cartels and systemic corruption within its political framework. The intersection of organized crime and state power has created a form of narco-authoritarianism, where the lines between the government and criminal enterprises are blurred, and violence becomes both a tool of control and a symptom of deeper systemic failure. This dynamic has hollowed out Mexico's democratic institutions, leaving a country where elections, policy decisions, and even basic governance are often dictated by the interests of cartels and complicit elites.

Drug cartels in Mexico wield immense power, not only as criminal organizations but as economic and political entities that rival, and in many cases surpass, the state in their ability to enforce authority. Through bribes, intimidation, and outright violence, cartels infiltrate all levels of government, from local police forces to federal agencies. Public officials, judges, and law enforcement officers face the constant threat of assassination if they do not cooperate, while those who comply often reap financial rewards. This has led to what many describe as a "narco-state," where the government operates in the shadow of cartel influence, unable or unwilling to challenge their dominance. The result is a nation where the rule of law is subverted, and democratic processes are reduced to a façade.

The erosion of democratic institutions in Mexico is not limited to cartel influence. Government corruption has become endemic, with political leaders often complicit in the very systems they claim to oppose. Public resources are siphoned off for personal gain, and accountability is virtually nonexistent. High-profile anti-corruption campaigns often serve as little more than political theater, targeting rivals while leaving systemic issues untouched. This environment of impunity further weakens public trust in institutions, creating a vicious cycle where citizens feel abandoned by the state and democracy is reduced to an empty promise.

Multinational corporations have exacerbated these issues by exploiting Mexico's instability and economic vulnerabilities. Trade agreements like NAFTA (and its successor, the USMCA) have opened the country to foreign investment, but the benefits have been unevenly distributed. While these agreements promise economic growth, they often come at the

36

expense of local communities, particularly in rural areas. Large-scale development projects, often backed by multinational corporations, displace indigenous peoples, destroy ecosystems, and exacerbate inequality. Meanwhile, the wealth generated by these projects rarely trickles down to the communities most affected by their impact. Instead, it flows to a small elite already insulated from the country's systemic violence and poverty.

Mexico's reliance on foreign investment has further entrenched inequality. In many cases, multinational corporations collaborate with corrupt officials to secure favorable terms, ignoring labor rights, environmental protections, and community consent. This dynamic mirrors the extractive practices seen in other parts of North America, where resource exploitation becomes a driver of displacement and marginalization. The displacement of rural communities often forces individuals into precarious labor conditions or migration, further destabilizing the social fabric.

Narco-authoritarianism and corporate exploitation are mutually reinforcing, creating a landscape where power and wealth are concentrated in the hands of a few while the majority are left to navigate a system designed to exclude them. The violence perpetrated by cartels is mirrored by the structural violence of poverty, displacement, and environmental degradation. Both forms of violence are rooted in the same logic: a prioritization of profit and power over people.

Despite these challenges, resistance persists. Grassroots movements led by indigenous communities, journalists, and human rights advocates continue to fight against the forces of corruption and exploitation. These movements face incredible risks, with activists and reporters often targeted for assassination. Yet their resilience underscores a profound truth: the fight for democracy and justice in Mexico is not over. The same systems that exploit and oppress can be dismantled, but it will require sustained effort, international solidarity, and a commitment to addressing the root causes of inequality and corruption.

Mexico's struggles are not isolated; they are deeply interconnected with global systems of power. Cartels operate with the complicity of international markets that demand their products. Multinational corporations exploit Mexico's resources while benefiting from trade agreements brokered by more powerful nations. Corruption flourishes in the shadow of global indifference, as wealthier countries prioritize their economic interests over the well-being of the Mexican people. To understand Mexico's challenges is to understand the ways in which local struggles are shaped by global forces, and the necessity of confronting both.

Shared Challenges Across North America

The three nations of North America, Canada, the United States, and Mexico, may have distinct political and cultural identities, but their fates are deeply intertwined, shaped by the forces of trade, corporate greed, and global power dynamics. The U.S., as the dominant economic and cultural force on the continent, exerts an outsized influence on its neighbors, exporting not only its consumer products and political ideologies but also the systemic flaws that plague its own democracy. Through trade agreements, corporate practices, and cultural exports, the United States has helped construct a framework where inequality, environmental degradation, and authoritarianism thrive across borders.

Trade agreements like NAFTA, and now the USMCA, exemplify this interconnectedness. These agreements were sold as pathways to economic prosperity, designed to foster cooperation and growth across North America. In practice, they have often entrenched inequality and exacerbated corporate power. For Canada, these agreements have facilitated the dominance of extractive industries, prioritizing resource exports to the U.S. over sustainable economic development. For Mexico, they have opened the floodgates for multinational corporations to exploit labor and resources, further destabilizing rural communities and widening the gap between the wealthy and the poor. While these agreements have generated significant profits for corporations, the benefits for ordinary citizens have been minimal, creating a shared dynamic of economic dispossession across the continent.

Corporate practices, many of them originating in or modeled after U.S. industries, have also played a central role in shaping the trajectories of Canada and Mexico. U.S. corporations often operate with impunity in both countries, extracting resources and exploiting labor with little accountability. Canadian mining companies, backed by U.S. investment and demand, devastate ecosystems in both Canada and Mexico, displacing indigenous communities and poisoning water supplies. Meanwhile, in Mexico, American agribusinesses have pushed out local farmers, driving migration and economic instability. These corporate practices not only prioritize profit over people but also erode national sovereignty, as governments bend to the will of multinational interests.

The rise of authoritarianism across North America is another shared challenge, driven by the interplay of corporate greed, environmental destruction, and weakened democratic institutions. In the U.S., the fusion of Christian nationalism, GOP extremism, and corporate influence has created a system where democracy is under siege. Canada faces its own authoritarian tendencies, as indigenous protests and environmental activism are met with state repression to protect corporate interests. Mexico, meanwhile, grapples with the dual threats of narco-authoritarianism and multinational exploitation, both of which weaken its democratic foundations. Across the continent, these dynamics reinforce each other, creating a feedback loop where power and wealth are concentrated in fewer hands while the rights and voices of ordinary citizens are systematically diminished.

Environmental destruction serves as a stark example of these interconnected challenges. The U.S.'s insatiable demand for oil, gas, and other natural resources drives extractive industries in both Canada and Mexico, with devastating consequences for ecosystems and communities. The tar sands of Alberta, the copper mines of Sonora, and the deforestation of Chiapas are all tied to the same global supply chains, feeding the energy and consumption habits of the United States. The environmental costs, pollution, habitat loss, and climate change, do not respect borders, impacting all three nations and beyond. The shared reliance on fossil fuels and resource extraction has locked North America into a cycle of environmental degradation that perpetuates inequality and fuels authoritarian policies to suppress dissent.

Culturally, the U.S. exports not only consumer products and entertainment but also its political ideologies and values. The rise of far-right movements, Christian nationalism, and corporate-backed authoritarianism in the U.S. has emboldened similar trends in Canada and Mexico. Far-right politicians in Canada have adopted rhetoric and strategies pioneered by their American counterparts, while Mexico's narco-authoritarianism is reinforced by the demand for illicit drugs in the U.S. and the flow of American weapons southward. This cultural and political export reinforces the shared dynamics of greed, corruption, and authoritarianism across borders.

The cross-border nature of these challenges highlights the need for a united front in addressing them. Environmental destruction in Canada impacts the entire continent, just as narco-violence in Mexico fuels instability that reaches across borders. The erosion of democratic norms in the U.S. emboldens authoritarian tendencies in its neighbors, creating a ripple effect that undermines democracy throughout North

America. These challenges are not isolated; they are mutually reinforcing, driven by the same forces of greed, exploitation, and indifference to human rights.

Despite these shared struggles, resistance is also a unifying force across the continent. Indigenous communities in Canada and Mexico, often the first to feel the impacts of environmental destruction and corporate exploitation, are leading movements to defend land and sovereignty. Grassroots activists in the U.S. are fighting voter suppression, climate inaction, and corporate greed, creating models of resistance that resonate beyond its borders. Journalists and human rights advocates in Mexico risk their lives to expose corruption and violence, offering a blueprint for courage and accountability in the face of overwhelming odds.

The shared challenges across North America underscore a simple but profound truth: no single nation can address these issues alone. The systems that exploit and oppress are deeply interconnected, and so too must be the efforts to dismantle them. Solidarity across borders is not just an ideal, it is a necessity. If North America is to overcome the forces of authoritarianism, environmental destruction, and corporate greed, its people must recognize their shared fate and work together to create a future that prioritizes justice, equity, and sustainability.

The Shared Fight for Democracy and Justice

Across North America, grassroots movements are rising to oppose the systems of oppression that have entrenched corporate greed, authoritarianism, and environmental destruction. From indigenous-led land defense to environmental activism and anti-corruption campaigns, these movements represent the frontlines of a continent-wide struggle for democracy and justice. Though these struggles are distinct in their local contexts, they are deeply interconnected, reflecting the shared challenges facing Canada, Mexico, and the United States. Together, they form the foundation of a united opposition that is essential to dismantling the systems that exploit and oppress.

Indigenous-led movements are among the most powerful and enduring forces of opposition across North America. In Canada, indigenous communities have long fought against resource extraction projects that threaten their lands, waters, and ways of life. From opposing pipeline expansions in British Columbia to defending sacred sites in Alberta, these movements highlight the fundamental contradiction between Canada's liberal image and its colonial practices. Indigenous land defenders not only oppose environmental destruction but also assert their sovereignty, challenging the very foundations of a political and economic system built on the dispossession of indigenous peoples.

In Mexico, indigenous communities are similarly at the forefront of opposition. They have been instrumental in challenging large-scale development projects, such as mega-mines and hydroelectric dams, that displace rural populations and destroy ecosystems. These movements are often met with violent repression, as corporations and government forces collude to silence dissent. Despite the risks, indigenous leaders continue to organize, drawing on centuries of opposition to colonialism to protect their land and culture. Their struggles are a testament to the resilience and strength of grassroots movements in the face of overwhelming odds.

In the United States, indigenous movements like Standing Rock's opposition to the Dakota Access Pipeline have galvanized a broader environmental justice movement. These efforts have drawn attention to the interconnectedness of environmental and social justice, emphasizing that the fight for clean water and a livable planet is inseparable from the fight for indigenous rights. The U.S. has also seen a surge in grassroots activism around issues like voting rights, racial justice, and labor organizing, all of which push back against the systemic inequalities reinforced by corporate and political elites.

Environmental activism is another unifying thread across the continent. In Canada, environmentalists and indigenous communities have joined forces to oppose the expansion of the tar sands and the construction of pipelines like Trans Mountain. In Mexico, activists have opposed deforestation and industrial pollution, often risking their lives in a country where environmental advocacy is met with lethal force. In the U.S., movements to combat climate change and transition to renewable energy have gained momentum, even as federal policies lag behind. These environmental struggles highlight the shared stakes of a warming planet, where the actions of one country have profound consequences for its neighbors.

Anti-corruption campaigns also play a critical role in opposing authoritarianism and corporate greed. In Mexico, investigative journalists and grassroots organizations work tirelessly to expose the collusion between cartels, corporations, and government officials. Their efforts often come at great personal risk, as Mexico remains one of the most dangerous countries in the world for journalists. In the U.S., watchdog groups and activists fight to uncover the influence of dark money in politics, while labor unions push back against corporate exploitation. In Canada, indigenous activists and environmentalists continue to call out government hypocrisy, demanding accountability for policies that prioritize profit over people.

What unites these movements across North America is the recognition that the systems they oppose, corporate greed, environmental destruction, and authoritarian governance, are not confined by borders. The pipelines built in Canada serve U.S. markets. The drug cartels operating in Mexico are fueled by American demand and supplied with American weapons. The trade agreements that displace rural communities in

Mexico and strip indigenous land rights in Canada are negotiated in Washington. These systems are deeply interconnected, and so too must be the opposition to them.

A united North American opposition is not just desirable, it is essential. The forces of greed and oppression thrive on division, exploiting national and regional differences to maintain their power. But solidarity across borders can undermine these strategies, creating a collective force that is greater than the sum of its parts. Indigenous movements in Canada, Mexico, and the U.S. can learn from and support one another, sharing strategies and amplifying each other's voices.

Environmental activists can coordinate their efforts to address the shared challenges of climate change and resource extraction. Anti-corruption campaigns can expose the transnational networks of power that perpetuate inequality and exploitation. Labor movements, too, can work collaboratively to push back against multinational corporations that exploit workers across all three nations.

This united opposition requires more than just shared goals; it demands shared action. Grassroots movements must build alliances across borders, recognizing that their struggles are interconnected and that their victories depend on one another. Citizens in all three countries must reject the false narratives that pit them against each other and instead focus on dismantling the systems that exploit them all. Governments may fail to address these challenges, but the people of North America have the power to create a future based on justice, equity, and sustainability.

The shared fight for democracy and justice is not an abstract ideal, it is a necessity. The systems of greed and oppression that dominate North America will not be dismantled overnight, but they can be dismantled. The indigenous land defenders, environmental activists, anti-corruption advocates,

44

and labor organizers leading this fight are showing us the way.
Their courage and resilience remind us that change is possible,
even in the face of overwhelming odds. Together, across
borders and beyond divisions, the people of North America
can reclaim their future.

~3

Europe

Orbán's Hungary, Meloni's Italy, and the Far-Right
Nationalist Surge

Europe is witnessing the resurgence of far-right
authoritarianism, cloaked in the rhetoric of nationalism and
cultural preservation. Leaders like Viktor Orbán in Hungary
and Giorgia Meloni in Italy have positioned themselves as
defenders of "traditional values" against what they portray as
the moral and cultural decay of liberal democracy. While their
language invokes patriotism and sovereignty, their policies
reveal an agenda that systematically undermines democratic
institutions, erodes civil liberties, and amplifies xenophobia.
These leaders are not isolated figures; they are part of a
broader far-right movement sweeping across Europe, fueled
by a combination of economic discontent, cultural anxiety,
and the deliberate weaponization of fear.

Viktor Orbán's Hungary stands as one of the clearest
examples of modern European fascism. Since returning to
power in 2010, Orbán has transformed Hungary into what he
proudly calls an "illiberal democracy." In practice, this means
consolidating power, dismantling checks and balances, and
reshaping the country's political and social fabric to serve his
authoritarian agenda. Orbán has systematically eroded
judicial independence, restricted press freedoms, and rewritten
election laws to ensure the dominance of his party, Fidesz. He
has weaponized nationalism to stoke fears of immigration,
portraying migrants, particularly those from Muslim-majority
countries, as existential threats to Hungary's identity and
security.

Orbán's cultural policies are equally insidious. His government
has pushed a narrative of "Christian values" to marginalize
LGBTQ+ communities, restrict women's rights, and promote

an exclusionary vision of Hungarian identity. Education, the arts, and media have all been co-opted to serve this narrative, with dissenting voices silenced through censorship or economic pressure. The result is a society where diversity is vilified, dissent is dangerous, and democracy exists only as a hollowed-out formality.

Giorgia Meloni's rise to power in Italy follows a similar trajectory, albeit with a more polished veneer. As the leader of the far-right Brothers of Italy party, Meloni has positioned herself as a modern, media-savvy nationalist, carefully distancing herself from the overt fascism of Italy's past while echoing its themes. Her rhetoric centers on defending Italian identity, family values, and sovereignty, often at the expense of marginalized groups. Immigrants, LGBTQ+ individuals, and women seeking reproductive rights have become targets of her policies and rhetoric, framed as threats to the traditional Italian way of life.

Meloni's government has also embraced authoritarian tactics, including crackdowns on press freedoms and attempts to reshape public institutions to align with her ideology. While her party officially disavows its fascist roots, its actions and alliances suggest otherwise. Meloni's emphasis on national identity and cultural purity echoes the playbook of far-right leaders across Europe, who exploit economic struggles and social anxieties to push exclusionary policies and consolidate power.

What makes leaders like Orbán and Meloni particularly dangerous is their ability to frame authoritarianism as a defense of democracy. By positioning themselves as champions of their nations' sovereignty, they cast their opponents, whether immigrants, political adversaries, or progressive activists, as enemies of the state. This strategy not only garners domestic support but also legitimizes their actions on the global stage, allowing them to erode democracy while claiming to protect it.

Far-right movements across Europe have taken note of their success, replicating their strategies to gain power in other countries. Parties like France's National Rally, Spain's Vox, and Germany's Alternative for Germany have adopted similar nationalist rhetoric, targeting immigrants, the LGBTQ+ community, and progressive movements as scapegoats for societal problems. These movements feed on economic insecurity, cultural fears, and a growing distrust of traditional political institutions, offering simple, exclusionary solutions to complex challenges. The result is a Europe where far-right nationalism is no longer confined to the fringes but has become a mainstream political force.

This nationalist surge is not just a European phenomenon; it has global implications. Leaders like Orbán and Meloni are forging alliances with far-right figures and parties around the world, sharing strategies and resources to promote their authoritarian agendas. Orbán, for example, has cultivated relationships with right-wing leaders in the United States, hosting events like the Conservative Political Action Conference (CPAC) in Budapest to strengthen transatlantic ties with far-right ideologues. Meloni, meanwhile, has positioned herself as a key figure in Europe's conservative resurgence, aligning with leaders like Poland's Andrzej Duda and fostering connections with far-right movements globally.

The rise of far-right nationalism in Europe under leaders like Orbán and Meloni is not an accident; it is the result of deliberate, calculated efforts to exploit fear and division for political gain. These leaders have mastered the art of manipulating democratic systems to undermine them from within, using the language of patriotism to disguise their authoritarian ambitions. As their influence spreads, the challenge for Europe and the world is clear: how to oppose this surge of far-right nationalism before it undermines democracy entirely.

Russia's Propaganda Machine and Putin's Global Fascist Export

Russia under Vladimir Putin represents one of the most potent forces for the export of authoritarianism and fascist ideology on the global stage. For over two decades, Putin has consolidated his power domestically by dismantling democratic institutions, silencing opposition, and weaponizing propaganda. But his ambitions extend far beyond Russia's borders. Through disinformation campaigns, strategic alliances, and ideological influence, Putin has worked to destabilize liberal democracies and promote a global resurgence of authoritarianism. In doing so, he has become a central figure in the global fascist movement, blending nationalism, imperialism, and autocracy into a toxic model that others seek to emulate.

At home, Putin's grip in Russia is built on a foundation of fear and control. Opposition figures are routinely jailed, exiled, or assassinated, and the press operates under strict state control. The Russian state manipulates public opinion through relentless propaganda, portraying Putin as a strongman defending the nation against foreign enemies and internal traitors. This narrative is reinforced by a deeply nationalist ideology that positions Russia as a bastion of traditional values under siege from the West. LGBTQ+ rights, feminism, and multiculturalism are demonized as Western imports designed to weaken Russia, while conservative, Orthodox Christian values are elevated as the essence of Russian identity.

This ideological framework is exported globally through a sophisticated disinformation apparatus. Russia's state-controlled media outlets, such as RT and Sputnik, serve as megaphones for pro-Kremlin narratives, amplifying division and mistrust in democracies around the world. These outlets don't just promote Russian interests; they actively undermine the credibility of democratic systems by spreading conspiracy theories, amplifying extremist voices, and exploiting societal fractures. By targeting elections, social movements, and public trust, Russia's propaganda machine sows chaos and weakens the cohesion of democratic societies.

One of the most striking examples of Russia's disinformation efforts was its interference in the 2016 U.S. presidential election, where Kremlin-backed trolls and bots spread false narratives to polarize the electorate and undermine faith in the democratic process. Similar tactics have been deployed across Europe, from supporting far-right parties in Germany to promoting Brexit in the United Kingdom. These efforts are not random but part of a calculated strategy to destabilize adversaries and create an international environment more favorable to authoritarianism.

Putin's export of fascist ideology extends beyond propaganda to strategic alliances with far-right movements and leaders worldwide. From Marine Le Pen's National Rally in France to Matteo Salvini's League in Italy, Russia has cultivated relationships with far-right parties that share its disdain for liberal democracy and its embrace of nationalism. These alliances are often transactional, with Russia providing financial support or strategic guidance in exchange for political influence. But they also reflect shared goals: the erosion of Western democratic norms, the promotion of authoritarian governance, and the establishment of a multipolar world order where power is concentrated in the hands of strongmen.

The war in Ukraine exemplifies Putin's imperialist ambitions and his willingness to use fascist tactics to achieve them. The invasion, framed as a "special military operation" to protect Russian speakers and denazify Ukraine, is a textbook example of authoritarian propaganda. The narrative is as false as it is dangerous, but it serves Putin's larger goal of reasserting Russia's dominance over its neighbors and challenging the post-Cold War global order. The war has been marked by atrocities, including the targeting of civilians, mass displacements, and the destruction of critical infrastructure, all hallmarks of a regime that prioritizes power over humanity.

Russia's actions in Ukraine have also emboldened other authoritarian regimes, offering a playbook for territorial aggression and internal suppression. The message is clear: if Russia can defy international law and democratic norms with relative impunity, so can others. This ripple effect extends to countries like China, where Putin's approach to propaganda and repression has found a receptive audience, and to far-right leaders in Europe, who view Russia's strongman politics as a model for their own aspirations.

Yet, Putin's authoritarianism is not invincible. His reliance on propaganda and coercion underscores the fragility of his regime, which depends on maintaining an illusion of strength and control. The growing resistance to his war in Ukraine, both within Russia and internationally, reveals cracks in the foundation of his power. The global response to the invasion, including economic sanctions, military support for Ukraine, and diplomatic isolation, demonstrates that collective opposition can challenge even the most entrenched autocracies.

Russia's role as a global exporter of fascist ideology is a stark reminder of the interconnected nature of modern authoritarianism. Putin's regime is not an outlier but part of a broader network of strongmen, far-right movements, and corporate interests that undermine democracy and human rights. To counter this network, the opposition must be equally global, rooted in solidarity and shared commitment to democratic values. The fight against Putin's Russia is not just about defending Ukraine or resisting propaganda; it is about confronting the global rise of authoritarianism before it reshapes the world into its image.

Russia's involvement in **BRICS** (Brazil, Russia, India, China, South Africa) highlights its strategic efforts to reshape global power dynamics in favor of authoritarian regimes. **BRICS**, originally an economic bloc aimed at challenging Western dominance in finance and trade, has become a tool for countries like Russia to undermine the liberal international order. By aligning with other authoritarian-leaning members like China, Putin leverages **BRICS** as a platform to weaken U.S. and European influence while promoting an alternative system that prioritizes state sovereignty over human rights and democracy.

Within **BRICS**, Russia plays a key role in initiatives such as the New Development Bank, which funds infrastructure projects in the Global South, and efforts to reduce reliance on the U.S. dollar in trade. While these measures are framed as empowering non-Western nations, they serve to consolidate the influence of authoritarian states. For non-**BRICS** countries, this poses significant challenges, as they may be pressured to align with competing blocs, undermining their sovereignty.

Russia's exploitation of **BRICS** also extends to its propaganda, framing itself as a champion of anti-colonialism and economic independence. However, this narrative obscures its real goal: reinforcing its geopolitical interests and authoritarian control. As **BRICS** grows, its capacity to bypass sanctions and reshape global trade rules threatens the existing checks on autocracies. The coalition's rise underscores the urgent need for democratic nations to respond, ensuring that principles of justice and human rights remain central to the global order.

~4
South America

Bolsonaro's Environmental Fascism and the Destruction of the Amazon

Under Jair Bolsonaro's presidency, Brazil became the epicenter of environmental fascism, where corporate greed and far-right authoritarianism collided to devastate the Amazon and its indigenous communities. Bolsonaro's regime prioritized the exploitation of natural resources over environmental preservation, dismantling decades of progress in safeguarding the world's largest rainforest. This was not simply a matter of economic policy, it was a deliberate project that weaponized nationalism, eroded indigenous rights, and subordinated the planet's health to corporate interests.

From the outset of his presidency, Bolsonaro made his intentions clear. He referred to the Amazon as an obstacle to Brazil's economic growth and dismissed environmental protections as unnecessary bureaucracy. His administration slashed funding for environmental enforcement agencies, fired scientists and experts who criticized his policies, and weakened laws that protected indigenous lands. This systematic dismantling of safeguards opened the floodgates for illegal logging, mining, and agribusiness expansion, much of it driven by global demand for soy, beef, and timber.

The role of corporate interests in this destruction cannot be overstated. Brazil's agribusiness sector, a powerful political force, reaped enormous profits from the expansion of agricultural frontiers into the Amazon. Multinational corporations, eager to capitalize on cheap resources, turned a blind eye to the illegal deforestation that fueled their supply chains. Bolsonaro's government facilitated this exploitation, not only by rolling back protections but by portraying environmentalists and indigenous communities as enemies of the state. Indigenous land defenders who resisted these incursions faced harassment, violence, and even assassination, often with impunity for the perpetrators.

The environmental consequences of Bolsonaro's policies are catastrophic. The Amazon, a vital carbon sink that regulates the Earth's climate, is being pushed toward a tipping point where it could transform into a savanna, releasing massive amounts of carbon into the atmosphere and accelerating global warming. The loss of biodiversity is equally devastating, with countless species at risk of extinction due to habitat destruction. For indigenous peoples, the stakes are existential: the Amazon is not only their home but their cultural and spiritual foundation. Bolsonaro's policies represent an existential threat to their way of life, erasing their sovereignty to make way for corporate profits.

Internationally, Bolsonaro's environmental fascism drew condemnation, but little meaningful action. Wealthier nations continued to import commodities tied to deforestation, and global financial institutions remained complicit by funding projects that contributed to the Amazon's destruction. While Bolsonaro may no longer be in office, the legacy of his environmental policies endures, as the systems of exploitation he nurtured are deeply embedded in Brazil's political and economic framework. The fight to save the Amazon is far from over, and it demands a global response that holds corporations and complicit governments accountable.

The destruction of the Amazon under Bolsonaro illustrates how authoritarian leaders and corporate interests work hand in hand to exploit natural resources at the expense of the planet and its people. It is a stark reminder that environmental justice and human rights are inseparable, and that the fight for one cannot succeed without the other. The Amazon is not just a Brazilian issue; it is a global imperative. The question is whether the world will rise to meet this challenge, or allow the greed of a few to determine the fate of many.

Venezuela's Authoritarian Grip and Colombia's Oligarchic Struggles

South America's political landscape reveals the intersection of authoritarianism, corporate exploitation, and entrenched inequality. In Venezuela, Nicolás Maduro's regime has turned the country into an archetype of modern authoritarian control, while Colombia grapples with the deep-rooted influence of oligarchic elites over its economy and politics. Both nations demonstrate how the concentration of power, whether through state dominance or elite control, creates systems that perpetuate oppression and inequality.

Venezuela, once one of South America's wealthiest nations, is now a case study in economic collapse and political authoritarianism. Nicolás Maduro, building on the foundation laid by his predecessor Hugo Chávez, has consolidated power through increasingly repressive means. Under the guise of socialist rhetoric, Maduro has gutted democratic institutions, silenced dissent, and relied on the military to maintain control. Elections are frequently manipulated, opposition leaders are jailed or exiled, and media outlets face severe restrictions, leaving little room for political plurality.

At the heart of Venezuela's crisis is its reliance on oil, which accounts for the majority of its economy. When global oil prices collapsed, the economy spiraled into chaos, exacerbated by government mismanagement and corruption. Maduro's regime has maintained its grip by exploiting the country's natural resources, granting lucrative extraction contracts to foreign corporations and allies like Russia and China. This resource-driven authoritarianism enriches a small elite while leaving the majority of Venezuelans to suffer through hyperinflation, food shortages, and deteriorating public services. The regime's use of economic hardship as a weapon, denying aid, hoarding resources, and punishing dissenters, has turned survival into a daily struggle for millions.

Colombia, while often held up as a more stable democracy, faces its own struggles rooted in the oligarchic control of its economy and politics. For decades, Colombia's political system has been dominated by a narrow elite, whose policies have prioritized corporate interests and foreign investment over the needs of its people. This dynamic has created one of the most unequal societies in Latin America, with wealth concentrated in the hands of a few while millions live in poverty.

The Colombian government's alignment with multinational corporations, particularly in industries like mining, agriculture, and energy, has driven widespread displacement and environmental destruction. Indigenous and Afro-Colombian communities are disproportionately affected, often forced off their lands to make way for resource extraction projects. The government's failure to address these injustices has fueled unrest and contributed to the persistence of armed conflict, even in the wake of the 2016 peace agreement with the FARC guerrilla group.

Colombia's struggles are compounded by the influence of paramilitary groups and drug cartels, which often operate with impunity. These groups not only perpetuate violence but also maintain ties to political and economic elites, creating a shadow network of power that undermines democracy. Activists and community leaders who oppose these systems face harassment, violence, and assassination, making Colombia one of the most dangerous countries in the world for human rights defenders.

Despite these challenges, both Venezuela and Colombia have seen growing opposition movements. In Venezuela, citizens continue to protest against Maduro's regime, even in the face of brutal crackdowns. International solidarity and humanitarian aid have provided some relief, but the path to meaningful change remains fraught with obstacles. In Colombia, grassroots organizations, indigenous movements, and labor unions are pushing back against oligarchic control, demanding greater accountability and equity. These efforts underscore the resilience of communities that refuse to accept the status quo.

The intertwined struggles of Venezuela and Colombia reflect a broader pattern in South America, where authoritarianism and oligarchy feed off one another, exploiting natural resources and human lives to sustain systems of power. The fight for justice in these countries is not only a local issue but part of a larger battle against the forces of greed and oppression that shape the region. As South America grapples with these challenges, the question remains: will these systems of control be dismantled, or will they continue to define the continent's future?

~5
Africa

Neocolonial Exploitation and the Plundering of Africa's Resources

Africa's vast wealth of natural resources has long been a double-edged sword, promising prosperity but delivering exploitation, conflict, and environmental devastation. The scars of colonialism remain deeply embedded in the continent's political and economic structures, perpetuated today through neocolonial systems of control. Global corporations, often backed by Western and Chinese interests, extract Africa's resources under the guise of development, leaving destruction in their wake. Nations like Congo and Angola epitomize how this exploitation sustains poverty, fuels corruption, and undermines sovereignty, all while enriching a global elite.

The Democratic Republic of Congo (DRC), one of the world's most resource-rich nations, is also one of its most exploited. The DRC's vast deposits of cobalt, copper, and gold are essential to global industries, particularly in the production of electronics and electric vehicles. Yet, despite this wealth, the Congolese people remain among the poorest in the world. Global corporations and local elites profit immensely from these resources, often at the expense of workers and communities. Artisanal miners, including children, labor under dangerous conditions for a pittance, while profits flow to multinational companies and corrupt government officials.

This neocolonial dynamic is facilitated by weak governance and systemic corruption, which allow foreign corporations to operate with impunity. Tax revenues from mining are minimal, as profits are funneled through offshore accounts and tax havens. Meanwhile, the environmental consequences of resource extraction, deforestation, polluted water sources, and degraded ecosystems, further impoverish local communities, who bear the brunt of these costs without reaping any benefits.

Angola tells a similar story. Rich in oil and diamonds, Angola's economy has been shaped by decades of exploitation and corruption. The ruling elite, centered around the authoritarian MPLA party, has used resource wealth to consolidate power while neglecting the needs of the broader population. The country's oil revenues, which account for a significant portion of its GDP, have been siphoned off to fund luxury lifestyles for government officials and their families. At the same time, ordinary Angolans face high unemployment, inadequate healthcare, and poor living conditions.

Global corporations play a central role in Angola's exploitation, partnering with the government to secure lucrative resource deals while turning a blind eye to human rights abuses and corruption. These partnerships perpetuate a cycle of dependency, where Angola's economy remains tied to resource extraction, leaving it vulnerable to price fluctuations and external pressures. This dependency reinforces authoritarian control, as the regime uses resource wealth to fund its security apparatus and suppress dissent.

The environmental toll of resource extraction in Angola is staggering. Oil spills, deforestation, and land degradation have displaced communities and destroyed livelihoods, compounding the social and economic inequalities entrenched by the regime. Yet, global corporations continue to frame their operations as investments in development, masking their role in perpetuating neocolonial exploitation.

Neocolonialism in Africa extends beyond resource extraction to include trade policies, debt traps, and geopolitical maneuvering. Countries like China have become major players in Africa, offering infrastructure loans and investments that come with steep political and economic costs. These arrangements often prioritize resource access for foreign

powers over the long-term needs of African nations, locking
them into cycles of debt and dependency.

The human cost of this exploitation is immense. Displaced
communities, environmental degradation, and systemic
poverty are not inevitable outcomes but the direct result of
policies and practices designed to prioritize profit over people.
Africa's resources are treated as commodities to be extracted,
rather than as foundations for sustainable development. This
system perpetuates the inequalities and injustices of
colonialism, repackaged for the modern era.

Despite these challenges, opposition is growing. Grassroots
movements, indigenous activists, and environmental advocates
across Africa are fighting to reclaim sovereignty over their
resources and demand accountability from both corporations
and governments. Their efforts highlight the urgent need for
systemic change, not only in Africa but in the global systems
that perpetuate exploitation. The question is whether the
world will continue to plunder Africa's wealth or finally
recognize its people's right to determine their own future.

Authoritarian Regimes/Extractive Industries Sustaining Them

Africa's wealth of natural resources has fueled neocolonial
exploitation and served as the backbone of authoritarian
regimes. In nations like Eritrea and Uganda, resource
extraction and foreign investment are deeply intertwined with
state power, sustaining repressive governments while
perpetuating inequality and environmental destruction. These
regimes exploit natural wealth to entrench control, repress
dissent, and maintain systems of oppression that benefit the
few at the expense of the many.

Eritrea stands as one of the most repressive states in the world,
ruled by Isaias Afwerki since its independence in 1993. Often
referred to as the "North Korea of Africa," Eritrea's

authoritarian grip is bolstered by its control over natural resources, particularly its mining industry. The government's partnerships with foreign mining companies, including Canadian and Chinese firms, have provided revenue that bypasses the population entirely. Profits are funneled into military expenditures and the regime's security apparatus, enforcing indefinite conscription and forced labor. The mining sector is notorious for conscripted labor, amounting to modern-day slavery, as Eritreans work under brutal conditions with no freedom to leave.

The environmental and social costs of mining in Eritrea are staggering, yet foreign companies continue to operate there, insulated from accountability by the regime's control. This exploitation fuels Afwerki's regime and global supply chains that depend on these materials, embedding Eritrea's role in the global system of oppression.

Uganda presents a different but equally troubling case. Under Yoweri Museveni, who has ruled since 1986, Uganda has become a textbook example of how resource wealth can sustain authoritarianism. Recent oil discoveries along Lake Albert have attracted significant foreign investment, with multinational corporations eager to exploit the reserves. Museveni's government has leveraged this newfound wealth to tighten its grip on power, using oil revenues to fund security forces and suppress opposition. Environmental concerns and the displacement of local communities have been disregarded, as the regime prioritizes foreign partnerships over the well-being of its people.

The construction of the East African Crude Oil Pipeline (EACOP), a joint venture involving Uganda, Tanzania, and international oil firms, illustrates the devastating intersection of resource extraction and authoritarian control. The pipeline, which threatens to displace thousands and damage critical ecosystems, has been met with widespread opposition from environmental and human rights groups. Yet the Museveni regime has dismissed these concerns, cracking down on activists and stifling dissent to push the project forward. The EACOP exemplifies how extractive industries in Africa not only degrade the environment but also empower regimes that rely on repression to maintain control.

Across the continent, the role of extractive industries in sustaining authoritarian regimes is a recurring theme. These governments use resource wealth to fund militarization, suppress political opposition, and entrench elite power structures. At the same time, foreign corporations profit immensely, enjoying access to Africa's resources without accountability for the environmental or human costs. This dynamic perpetuates cycles of exploitation and inequality, leaving local populations to bear the brunt of environmental degradation, displacement, and poverty.

Resistance to these systems is growing, led by activists, communities, and international organizations demanding change. In Uganda, environmental groups have rallied against the EACOP, highlighting its devastating impacts and the complicity of foreign firms. In Eritrea, exiled activists and human rights organizations work tirelessly to expose the regime's abuses and advocate for international action. These movements, though facing immense challenges, represent the possibility of a future where Africa's resources are managed equitably and sustainably.

The extractive industries that sustain authoritarian regimes in Africa are not inevitable; they are the result of deliberate policies and global complicity. Addressing these systems requires more than reform, it demands a fundamental shift in how the world views and interacts with Africa. Resource wealth should be a source of empowerment, not oppression. The fight for justice in Eritrea, Uganda, and across the continent is not just Africa's struggle, it is a global imperative to dismantle the systems that exploit and oppress.

6

Asia

China's Surveillance State and the Export of Digital Authoritarianism

China's rise as a global superpower has been accompanied by the construction of one of the most comprehensive and invasive surveillance states in history. Under the leadership of Xi Jinping, the Chinese government has leveraged advanced technologies to monitor, control, and suppress its population while exporting its model of digital authoritarianism to other countries. What makes China's approach particularly insidious is its ability to present this system as a tool for efficiency and security, disguising its true purpose: the consolidation of state power and the eradication of dissent.

At home, China's surveillance state is omnipresent. The government has deployed millions of surveillance cameras equipped with facial recognition technology, creating an infrastructure that tracks individuals in real time. This system is integrated with data from smartphones, social media, and financial transactions, allowing authorities to build detailed profiles of every citizen. Combined with the "Social Credit System," which rewards or punishes behavior based on government-defined standards, this surveillance apparatus enables an unprecedented level of social control. Citizens deemed loyal to the state are rewarded, while those who criticize the government face consequences ranging from travel restrictions to job loss or imprisonment.

The Uyghur Muslim population in the Xinjiang region provides the most chilling example of China's surveillance capabilities. The region has become a testing ground for advanced surveillance technologies, including AI-driven behavior monitoring and predictive policing. The Chinese government has used these tools to facilitate the mass internment of Uyghurs in "re-education camps," where detainees face forced labor, indoctrination, and abuse. This level of oppression would be impossible without the technological infrastructure that tracks and monitors every aspect of Uyghur life, from biometric data collection to AI-powered voice analysis. The scale of this operation underscores the authoritarian ambition of the Chinese state, which seeks to erase dissent and cultural identity under the guise of stability.

China's surveillance state is not confined to its borders. Through its Belt and Road Initiative, the Chinese government has exported its digital authoritarianism to countries across Asia, Africa, and beyond. By providing surveillance technologies, infrastructure, and training to authoritarian-leaning governments, China has enabled other regimes to suppress dissent and maintain control. Nations like Cambodia, Zimbabwe, and even some Gulf states have adopted Chinese surveillance systems to monitor activists, journalists, and political opponents, demonstrating the global reach of China's model. The appeal of these systems lies in their ability to offer governments enhanced control over their populations, turning surveillance into a form of soft power for Beijing.

The export of digital authoritarianism is further facilitated by Chinese tech giants like Huawei and ZTE. These companies, closely tied to the Chinese state, supply governments with the tools needed to build their own surveillance infrastructures. While marketed as tools for urban planning or crime prevention, these technologies are often used to target dissidents and suppress opposition. By embedding itself in the digital ecosystems of other countries, China extends its influence while normalizing the use of technology for authoritarian purposes. In essence, China is not merely exporting technology but exporting a worldview where surveillance and control are paramount.

The implications of China's surveillance state and its export of digital authoritarianism extend to the global stage. By promoting its model, China is reshaping international norms around governance, privacy, and human rights. In multilateral forums, Chinese representatives advocate for policies that prioritize state control over internet freedom, undermining the open and decentralized nature of the web. The result is a fragmented digital landscape, where authoritarian regimes wield technology to consolidate power while restricting dissent. This shift risks normalizing a future in which surveillance, rather than transparency, becomes the cornerstone of governance.

The challenge posed by China's surveillance state is not just about technology, it's about the values that underpin its use. The tools themselves are neutral, but their application determines whether they liberate or oppress. As China exports its model of digital authoritarianism, democratic nations must act decisively to counter its spread. This means holding tech companies accountable, supporting civil society initiatives that promote digital privacy, and working toward global frameworks that prioritize individual rights over state control. The stakes could not be higher. If unchecked, China's model could set a precedent for the rest of the world, creating a future where freedom is sacrificed at the altar of control.

Special Note: Taiwan – A Flashpoint in the Fight Against Authoritarianism

Taiwan represents one of the most urgent and high-stakes battlegrounds in the global struggle against authoritarianism. Claimed by China as an inseparable part of its territory, Taiwan's democratic government and thriving economy stand in direct defiance of Beijing's authoritarian ambitions. Under Xi Jinping, China has escalated its campaign to "reunify" Taiwan with the mainland, deploying military threats, diplomatic isolation, and economic coercion to undermine the island's sovereignty. This conflict is not only about Taiwan's future but also about the survival of democratic ideals in the face of authoritarian expansionism.

China's ambitions toward Taiwan reflect a broader strategy of territorial and ideological control. Military posturing, including frequent incursions into Taiwan's air defense identification zone (ADIZ) and large-scale naval exercises, has become a near-daily reality for the island. Beijing portrays these actions as routine, but they are part of a deliberate campaign to intimidate Taiwan and test the resolve of its allies, particularly the United States. Xi has repeatedly refused to rule out the use of force, making the possibility of war increasingly tangible.

Taiwan's strategic significance amplifies the stakes. As a global leader in semiconductor manufacturing, Taiwan plays a critical role in the world's technology supply chains. Its geographic position also makes it a key player in regional security in the Indo-Pacific. The United States, bound by the Taiwan Relations Act, supports Taiwan's self-defense and has recently increased arms sales and diplomatic engagement. However, the U.S. policy of "strategic ambiguity" leaves open questions about how far it would go to defend Taiwan in the event of Chinese aggression.

The potential for conflict over Taiwan carries global consequences. A war would destabilize the Indo-Pacific region, disrupt global trade, and potentially draw in major powers like the United States, Japan, and Australia. Taiwan is more than a geopolitical flashpoint; it is a test case for whether democracies can withstand the growing tide of authoritarianism. How the world responds to Taiwan's struggle will set the tone for the broader fight against authoritarian expansion in the 21st century.

India's Hindu Nationalism Under Modi and Southeast Asia's Struggles Against Military Rule

India under Narendra Modi has seen a dramatic rise in Hindu nationalism, transforming the country's secular foundations into a battleground for religious and cultural supremacy. Modi and his Bharatiya Janata Party (BJP) have reshaped Indian politics and society by fusing authoritarian governance with a vision of Hindu primacy. This ideology, known as Hindutva, seeks to redefine India as a Hindu nation, marginalizing its religious minorities, especially Muslims, and eroding its democratic institutions. Meanwhile, Southeast Asia faces its own authoritarian challenges, with military juntas and repressive regimes suppressing dissent and exploiting their people. From India to Myanmar, the rise of authoritarianism in Asia represents a coordinated assault on democracy and human rights.

Modi's government has steadily dismantled India's secular and pluralistic ideals, using religious polarization as a political tool. Policies such as the Citizenship Amendment Act (CAA) have institutionalized discrimination against Muslims, while incidents of mob violence and lynching, often targeting Muslims and Dalits, have become alarmingly frequent. Modi's supporters frame these actions as necessary to preserve India's identity, portraying religious minorities as threats to national unity. The government has further silenced opposition by weaponizing sedition and anti-terror laws, targeting activists, journalists, and academics critical of its policies. Major media outlets, often beholden to corporate interests aligned with the BJP, echo government narratives, leaving little room for dissent.

The digital landscape in India has also become a site of authoritarian control. The Modi government has increasingly used internet shutdowns, surveillance, and social media regulations to stifle protests and monitor critics. Kashmir, long

71

a disputed territory, has been a focal point of these tactics. After revoking Article 370 in 2019, which granted Jammu and Kashmir special autonomy, the government deployed troops, imposed curfews, and cut off internet access for months, turning the region into one of the most heavily militarized zones in the world. This crackdown exemplifies how Hindu nationalism is used to justify authoritarian policies, framing oppression as a matter of national security.

Southeast Asia faces parallel struggles, with military juntas and autocratic regimes suppressing democracy and perpetuating violence. Myanmar, once a beacon of hope for democratic transition, has descended into chaos since the military coup of 2021. The junta has brutally cracked down on protesters, journalists, and opposition leaders, killing thousands and displacing hundreds of thousands more. The Rohingya genocide, which began before the coup, continues unabated, as the military targets this Muslim minority for ethnic cleansing. The international community's muted response has emboldened the junta, which relies on resource exploitation and foreign partnerships to sustain its rule.

The situation in Myanmar is mirrored in varying degrees across Southeast Asia, where authoritarianism thrives under the guise of stability and development. In Thailand, the military has entrenched its power through repeated coups, suppressing dissent with harsh lèse majesté laws that criminalize criticism of the monarchy. Cambodia's Hun Sen, in power for nearly four decades, has systematically dismantled opposition parties and civil society organizations, turning the country into a one-party state. In the Philippines, Rodrigo Duterte's presidency was marked by a violent "war on drugs" that claimed thousands of lives, disproportionately affecting the poor and marginalized. While Duterte is no longer in power, the culture of impunity he fostered continues to shape the country's political landscape.

Throughout Southeast Asia, extractive industries and foreign investments play a critical role in sustaining authoritarian regimes. In Myanmar, the military profits from jade and timber exports, while in Cambodia, Chinese-backed infrastructure projects displace local communities and deepen the government's dependence on Beijing. These economic arrangements, often framed as development, serve to entrench inequality and bolster authoritarian control. The people most affected, indigenous communities, laborers, and activists, face immense risks when they oppose these systems.

Despite these challenges, resistance movements across Asia are refusing to back down. In India, farmers staged one of the largest protests in history, forcing Modi to repeal controversial agricultural laws. Activists continue to fight for secularism, women's rights, and environmental protections, even in the face of increasing repression. In Myanmar, the Civil Disobedience Movement (CDM) has united workers, students, and ethnic minorities against the military junta, demonstrating extraordinary resilience despite brutal crackdowns. Across Southeast Asia, pro-democracy movements, labor unions, and grassroots organizations are challenging authoritarian regimes, often at great personal cost.

The rise of Hindu nationalism and military rule in Asia highlights a disturbing trend: the use of identity, fear, and resource exploitation to justify authoritarianism. Yet, the region's resistance movements offer a powerful counter-narrative, one that emphasizes solidarity, justice, and the fight for self-determination. These struggles remind us that authoritarianism is not inevitable, it is the product of deliberate choices that can be challenged and undone. While the road ahead is fraught with danger, the courage of those who oppose these regimes offers hope for a more just and democratic Asia. If the people of India, Myanmar, and Southeast Asia can persist in their struggles, they may yet inspire a global movement to reclaim democracy and human rights from the grip of authoritarianism.

7

The Oceania and Global Consequences

Australia's Climate Fascism, Resource Exploitation, and the Suppression of Indigenous Voices

Australia, often lauded as a progressive democracy, reveals its darker side when viewed through the lens of climate fascism, resource exploitation, and its treatment of Indigenous communities. Despite its global image as an environmentally conscious nation, Australia remains one of the world's largest exporters of coal and natural gas, contributing disproportionately to climate change. Successive Australian governments, both conservative and centrist, have prioritized resource extraction over environmental sustainability and human rights, cementing the country's role as a major player in global ecological destruction. At the heart of this exploitation lies the systematic suppression of Indigenous voices and sovereignty, further exposing the authoritarian underpinnings of Australia's resource-driven economy.

Australia's economy has long been tied to its vast natural resources, including coal, iron ore, and natural gas. These industries wield enormous influence over the nation's politics, dictating policies that favor extraction at the expense of environmental protections. The government's close ties to the fossil fuel sector are evident in its reluctance to adopt meaningful climate policies. Despite international pressure and worsening climate crises, including devastating bushfires and coral bleaching in the Great Barrier Reef, Australia remains a steadfast defender of coal and gas exports. These policies reflect a form of climate fascism, where short-term economic gains for a privileged few are prioritized over the long-term survival of the planet and its most vulnerable communities.

The impact of resource exploitation is most acutely felt by Australia's Indigenous peoples, whose lands are often at the center of mining and extraction projects. Indigenous communities have consistently opposed these developments, citing the destruction of sacred sites, the degradation of ecosystems, and the loss of cultural heritage. However, their resistance is met with systematic suppression. Governments and corporations work hand in hand to marginalize Indigenous voices, using legal frameworks, economic pressures, and even law enforcement to silence opposition. For example, in the infamous case of Juukan Gorge in 2020, Rio Tinto destroyed a 46,000-year-old sacred site to expand an iron ore mine, sparking outrage but little tangible accountability.

Australia's approach to resource exploitation mirrors colonial dynamics, where Indigenous sovereignty is disregarded, and land is seen as a commodity to be extracted rather than a sacred trust to be preserved. Indigenous leaders and activists have long called for meaningful recognition of their rights and the protection of their lands, but these calls are often ignored or undermined. The result is a system where the benefits of resource extraction flow to multinational corporations and the political elite, while the costs, environmental, cultural, and human, are borne by Indigenous communities.

Australia's climate policies, or lack thereof, also exemplify a broader trend of environmental injustice. While the country's per capita emissions are among the highest in the world, it has done little to transition to renewable energy or support global climate efforts. Instead, Australia exports its environmental destruction, shipping coal and gas to nations like China and India, where they contribute to global emissions. This "out of sight, out of mind" approach allows Australia to shirk responsibility for its role in the climate crisis, framing itself as a victim of international criticism rather than a perpetrator of ecological harm.

The suppression of Indigenous voices in Australia is not just a domestic issue; it has global implications. As the world

76

grapples with the twin crises of climate change and environmental degradation, Indigenous communities offer invaluable knowledge and perspectives on sustainable living. By marginalizing these voices, Australia not only perpetuates injustice but also deprives the world of potential solutions. Indigenous resistance to resource exploitation is not merely a fight for survival, it is a fight for a more equitable and sustainable future.

Australia's climate fascism and resource-driven policies are a stark reminder of how economic interests can override environmental and human rights concerns. The country's actions have ripple effects far beyond its borders, contributing to global emissions, fueling ecological destruction, and undermining efforts to address the climate crisis. To understand the full scope of authoritarianism in Oceania, one must start with Australia's role as a willing participant in the exploitation of both its land and its people.

The Broader Environmental and Geopolitical Consequences of Fascist Policies in Oceania

The consequences of Oceania's fascist-leaning climate and resource policies extend far beyond the borders of Australia and its Pacific neighbors, creating a ripple effect that exacerbates global environmental and geopolitical challenges. Oceania, as a region, holds critical importance in the fight against climate change and in maintaining geopolitical stability. However, the authoritarian tendencies driving resource exploitation and environmental neglect have set the stage for cascading crises that will shape the future of the planet and its people.

At the heart of the region's global impact is Australia's status as one of the largest exporters of fossil fuels, including coal and liquefied natural gas (LNG). The unchecked expansion of these industries fuels global greenhouse gas emissions, driving the planet closer to climate tipping points. While Australia profits from the extraction and export of these resources, the climate devastation disproportionately impacts the Global South and vulnerable island nations in Oceania itself. Countries like Tuvalu, Kiribati, and the Marshall Islands are already experiencing rising sea levels that threaten their very existence, a crisis directly tied to the fossil fuel-driven policies of larger nations like Australia.

These environmental consequences are compounded by geopolitical tensions. The Pacific islands, many of which face existential threats from climate change, have become a battleground for influence between global powers like China and the United States. China's Belt and Road Initiative has extended its reach into the Pacific, providing infrastructure investments and loans to island nations. While these partnerships are framed as development opportunities, they often come with hidden costs, including debt traps and growing political dependency on Beijing. This dynamic fuels instability in the region, as smaller nations are forced to navigate between competing superpowers while grappling with the immediate impacts of climate change.

Australia, rather than acting as a stabilizing force, has often exacerbated these tensions. Despite being a regional power, its climate inaction and refusal to prioritize renewable energy have undermined its credibility among its Pacific neighbors. Nations like Fiji and Samoa have repeatedly called out Australia's hypocrisy, condemning its role in perpetuating the climate crisis while offering limited support to those bearing the brunt of its effects. This erosion of trust has weakened Australia's influence in the region, creating openings for other actors, particularly China, to expand their foothold.

The suppression of Indigenous voices and land rights within Australia has global implications as well. The wisdom and practices of Indigenous communities, who have sustainably managed ecosystems for millennia, offer critical insights into combating climate change and biodiversity loss. By marginalizing these voices, Australia not only perpetuates injustice at home but also squanders opportunities to lead the world in climate solutions rooted in Indigenous knowledge and environmental stewardship. The global community suffers as these perspectives are systematically excluded from decision-making processes.

Geopolitically, the climate crisis and resource-driven exploitation in Oceania are reshaping alliances and power dynamics. The United States, seeking to counter China's growing influence in the Pacific, has increased its engagement with island nations, offering aid and security partnerships. However, these efforts often fall short of addressing the root causes of the crisis, focusing instead on military presence and strategic advantage. The result is a region caught in the crossfire of global competition, where the voices of its most vulnerable inhabitants are overshadowed by the interests of larger powers.

The broader implications of Oceania's policies highlight the interconnectedness of environmental and geopolitical issues in the age of climate change. The choices made by nations like Australia reverberate far beyond their borders, shaping global emissions, international power structures, and the survival of entire communities. Addressing these challenges requires a rethinking of priorities, one that centers sustainability, equity, and the voices of those most affected. Oceania stands as both a warning and an opportunity: a region where the consequences of climate fascism are starkly visible, but where meaningful change could chart a new path for the world.

Section 2
Industries of Oppression

~8
Tech

Silicon Valley Billionaires, Techno-Fascism, and the Rise of Algorithmic Control

The rise of Silicon Valley billionaires as global power brokers has fundamentally reshaped modern society, concentrating unprecedented levels of wealth and influence in the hands of a small elite. Companies founded by figures like Mark Zuckerberg, Elon Musk, Jeff Bezos, and Sundar Pichai have not only revolutionized technology but also redefined the boundaries of governance, culture, and human agency. While these titans of industry present themselves as innovators and visionaries, their actions have fostered a new form of authoritarianism: techno-fascism. Through the use of algorithms, data collection, and artificial intelligence (AI), they have replaced human decision-making with opaque systems designed to maximize profit and control. This shift has undermined democracy, eroded privacy, and entrenched inequality, transforming the promise of technological advancement into a dystopian reality.

At the core of techno-fascism is the replacement of human agency with algorithmic control. Platforms like Facebook, Instagram, and YouTube employ algorithms that decide what content users see, tailoring feeds to maximize engagement and, by extension, advertising revenue. These algorithms are not neutral; they are designed to exploit human psychology, prioritizing sensationalism, outrage, and division over nuance and truth. By determining what information is amplified or suppressed, Silicon Valley's platforms wield immense power over public discourse, shaping opinions, elections, and even social movements.

The consequences of algorithmic control extend far beyond social media. In the realm of e-commerce, companies like Amazon use algorithms to manipulate consumer behavior, steering customers toward specific products and squeezing out competition. In the workplace, algorithms increasingly determine hiring, promotions, and even layoffs, replacing human judgment with automated systems that are often riddled with bias. In law enforcement, predictive policing algorithms claim to identify high-crime areas but frequently reinforce systemic racism, targeting marginalized communities while ignoring structural inequalities. These applications reveal the true nature of techno-fascism: a system that prioritizes efficiency and profit over fairness, accountability, and human dignity.

Silicon Valley billionaires have justified these practices with the rhetoric of progress and innovation, framing their actions as necessary for societal advancement. Yet, their decisions often reflect a ruthless pursuit of profit and power. Mark Zuckerberg's Facebook, for instance, has faced repeated scandals over its role in spreading misinformation, amplifying hate speech, and undermining democratic processes. Despite public outcry and regulatory scrutiny, Facebook's business model remains unchanged, prioritizing engagement metrics over the well-being of its users. Similarly, Elon Musk's ventures into AI and space exploration, while framed as ambitious solutions to humanity's problems, are driven by a vision that prioritizes technological dominance over ethical considerations.

The concentration of power in Silicon Valley has also created a feedback loop that reinforces techno-fascism. The wealth generated by these companies is used to fund lobbying efforts, ensuring that governments remain unwilling or unable to regulate their activities. At the same time, tech billionaires

82

have established themselves as arbiters of public policy, using their platforms and influence to shape debates on everything from free speech to climate change. This dynamic has blurred the line between corporate and governmental power, creating a system where unelected billionaires wield more influence than elected officials.

Perhaps the most insidious aspect of techno-fascism is its reliance on data collection and surveillance. Every interaction on digital platforms generates data, which is harvested, analyzed, and monetized by tech companies. This practice, known as surveillance capitalism, has turned personal information into the most valuable commodity of the digital age. Platforms like Google and Facebook track users across the internet, building detailed profiles that include everything from browsing habits to location data. This data is then used to target advertisements, predict behavior, and, in some cases, manipulate outcomes. The Cambridge Analytica scandal, where Facebook data was used to influence elections, is just one example of how surveillance capitalism can be weaponized for political and economic gain.

Surveillance capitalism also enables a level of control that would have been unthinkable just a few decades ago. Governments and corporations alike use data to monitor and influence populations, blurring the line between public and private surveillance. In China, for example, tech companies collaborate with the state to implement systems like facial recognition and social credit scoring, creating a society where every action is tracked and judged. While the U.S. lacks an official social credit system, Silicon Valley's practices reflect a similar logic, where data-driven algorithms determine access to opportunities, services, and even justice.

The implications of techno-fascism extend beyond individual rights to the very fabric of democracy. The manipulation of public discourse through social media monopolies has undermined trust in institutions, eroded social cohesion, and created fertile ground for authoritarian ideologies. Platforms like Twitter and YouTube amplify extremist content, polarizing communities and normalizing hate speech. At the same time, censorship practices, whether driven by corporate policies or state pressure, have raised concerns about the boundaries of free expression. The result is a digital landscape where misinformation thrives, dissent is stifled, and democratic norms are increasingly difficult to uphold.

This manipulation of discourse is not accidental; it is a feature of the system. Social media platforms are designed to keep users engaged, regardless of the content that achieves this goal. Outrage, conspiracy theories, and emotional appeals are more engaging than measured analysis, making them the currency of the digital age. This dynamic has had profound consequences, from the rise of populist leaders to the spread of anti-science movements. By prioritizing engagement over truth, Silicon Valley has created an environment where the loudest, most divisive voices dominate.

The concentration of power in the hands of Silicon Valley billionaires has also reshaped the global economy, exacerbating inequality and displacing workers. Automation, driven by advances in AI, has eliminated jobs across industries, from manufacturing to retail. While tech leaders frame automation as inevitable, they often ignore its human cost, dismissing displaced workers as collateral damage in the march of progress. At the same time, the gig economy, epitomized by companies like Uber and DoorDash, has created a class of precarious workers who lack basic protections and benefits. These trends reveal the true face of techno-fascism: a system that prioritizes efficiency and profit over human welfare.

Silicon Valley's influence is not confined to the digital realm; it extends into the physical world through initiatives like smart cities and the Internet of Things (IoT). While these projects promise to improve urban living through data-driven solutions, they also raise concerns about surveillance, privacy, and accountability. Smart city technologies, such as connected cameras and sensors, create new opportunities for monitoring and control, often without adequate safeguards or transparency. These systems risk entrenching existing inequalities, as the communities most affected by surveillance are often those with the least power to resist it.

The rise of techno-fascism is not inevitable, but it is deeply entrenched. Silicon Valley billionaires have built systems that prioritize profit over people, efficiency over ethics, and control over accountability. By replacing human agency with algorithms, they have created a world where decisions are made not by communities or institutions but by opaque systems designed to maximize shareholder value. This shift has profound implications for democracy, human rights, and the future of society, raising urgent questions about who benefits from technological progress and at what cost.

To address the challenges posed by techno-fascism, we must recognize the role of Silicon Valley billionaires in creating and perpetuating this system. Their decisions have shaped the digital landscape in ways that prioritize profit and control, undermining the values of fairness, transparency, and accountability. As these individuals continue to wield disproportionate influence over society, the need for regulation, oversight, and collective action has never been greater. The battle against techno-fascism is a battle for the soul of reality itself, a fight to ensure that technology serves humanity rather than oppressing it. The stakes could not be higher.

Surveillance Capitalism, Censorship, and the Manipulation of Public Discourse

Surveillance capitalism has become the defining economic model of the digital age, shaping how information is collected, monetized, and weaponized by tech companies. This model is rooted in the relentless extraction of personal data, transforming every action, whether searching, shopping, or simply existing online, into a commodifiable resource. In doing so, Silicon Valley companies like Google, Facebook, and Amazon have created systems of control that erode individual autonomy, compromise privacy, and foster authoritarian tendencies. At the heart of this system lies a chilling reality: these companies have unprecedented power to shape what people see, believe, and ultimately, how they act.

Surveillance capitalism thrives on the illusion of choice. Users voluntarily hand over data in exchange for convenience, entertainment, or utility, unaware of the extensive profiling that takes place behind the scenes. Every click, scroll, and interaction is recorded, analyzed, and fed into machine-learning algorithms that predict and influence future behavior. These predictive models are sold to advertisers, governments, and other entities, creating a multibillion-dollar industry that depends on constant surveillance. The more data collected, the more precise the predictions, and the greater the power wielded by those who control the systems.

This economic model is inseparable from the rise of social media monopolies, which have turned the manipulation of public discourse into a central feature of their platforms. Companies like Facebook and Twitter have become the primary arenas for political and social conversations, but their algorithms are designed not for informed debate but for engagement. Engagement, in this context, means time spent on the platform, and nothing drives engagement like outrage, fear, and division. Content that polarizes users, stirs emotions, or confirms biases is amplified, creating echo chambers that reinforce existing beliefs and drive users further into ideological extremes.

This manipulation of discourse has had profound consequences for democracy and social cohesion. Misinformation spreads faster than truth on platforms optimized for engagement, fueling conspiracy theories, anti-science movements, and extremist ideologies. The 2016 U.S. presidential election and the Brexit referendum highlighted how social media could be weaponized to distort democratic processes. Both events were marked by targeted disinformation campaigns, often funded by foreign actors, that exploited social media algorithms to sow division and influence outcomes. Despite public outrage and calls for reform, the platforms responsible for enabling these campaigns have largely avoided meaningful accountability.

The role of social media in amplifying hate speech and enabling authoritarian regimes is another dark facet of surveillance capitalism. In countries like Myanmar, Facebook has been directly implicated in the incitement of violence against the Rohingya Muslim population. The platform's algorithms amplified hate speech and dehumanizing rhetoric, fueling ethnic tensions and contributing to what the United Nations has called a genocide. Similar patterns can be seen in India, where platforms have been used to spread Hindu nationalist propaganda and incite violence against religious minorities. These examples reveal how the profit-driven logic of surveillance capitalism aligns with authoritarian interests, creating systems that perpetuate violence and oppression.

Censorship also plays a key role in the manipulation of public discourse, but it operates in complex and often contradictory ways. On one hand, governments and corporations pressure platforms to remove content deemed harmful, leading to concerns about free speech and overreach. On the other hand, these same platforms are slow to act against hate speech, misinformation, and harassment, particularly when such content drives engagement. The result is a patchwork of inconsistent policies that prioritize corporate interests over public good, leaving users vulnerable to both censorship and exploitation.

The privatization of information control raises troubling questions about accountability. Decisions about what content to promote, suppress, or remove are made not by democratically accountable institutions but by tech companies motivated by profit. These decisions often lack transparency, and users have little recourse when they are affected. This dynamic has led to a growing distrust of both social media platforms and the institutions that rely on them, further eroding public confidence in democratic systems.

The global reach of surveillance capitalism and social media monopolies has also enabled the export of techno-fascism. Authoritarian governments around the world have adopted Silicon Valley's tools to monitor dissent, suppress opposition, and maintain control. In countries like China and Saudi Arabia, social media platforms are used as instruments of state power, tracking activists and spreading propaganda. Even in democracies, the line between private and state surveillance is increasingly blurred, as governments collaborate with tech companies to access data and enforce control. This convergence of corporate and state interests represents a profound threat to individual freedoms and democratic norms.

The consequences of surveillance capitalism and techno-fascism extend beyond politics to the very fabric of society. By prioritizing profit and control over truth and transparency, Silicon Valley has created a system that thrives on division and distrust. Communities are fragmented, institutions are delegitimized, and individuals are left isolated and powerless in the face of algorithms they cannot understand or influence. This erosion of social cohesion creates fertile ground for authoritarian ideologies, which exploit fear and uncertainty to consolidate power.

Efforts to challenge surveillance capitalism and its effects have faced significant obstacles. Tech companies have invested heavily in lobbying and public relations campaigns to resist regulation, framing themselves as engines of innovation and economic growth. Meanwhile, whistleblowers and activists who expose the harms of these systems often face retaliation, further discouraging opposition. Despite these challenges, movements for digital rights, data privacy, and platform accountability are gaining momentum, highlighting the growing recognition that the current system is unsustainable.

One potential avenue for reform lies in rethinking the ownership and governance of digital platforms. Proposals for public or cooperative ownership of social media, where decisions are guided by public interest rather than profit, offer an alternative to the monopoly-driven model. Similarly, stronger data privacy laws, such as the European Union's General Data Protection Regulation (GDPR), can help limit the power of surveillance capitalism. However, these measures alone are not enough; addressing the root causes of techno-fascism requires a broader cultural shift that prioritizes human agency, accountability, and equity over efficiency and profit.

The stakes in the fight against surveillance capitalism and techno-fascism could not be higher. These systems have reshaped how we communicate, govern, and understand the world, concentrating power in the hands of a few while eroding the foundations of democracy and human rights. The path forward will require collective action, innovation, and a commitment to reclaiming technology as a force for liberation rather than oppression. The question is not whether these systems can be changed but whether society is willing to demand the change that is so desperately needed.

~ 9

Energy & Climate

Fossil Fuel Giants, Climate Denial, and the Rise of Resource-Driven Authoritarianism

The fossil fuel industry has long been a driving force behind some of the most destructive geopolitical and environmental trends of the modern era. From climate denial campaigns to enabling authoritarian regimes, fossil fuel giants wield power that shapes economies, politics, and public opinion on a global scale. While these corporations often frame themselves as indispensable providers of energy and economic stability, their actions reveal a pattern of exploitation, manipulation, and environmental devastation. This chapter explores how fossil fuel companies perpetuate climate denial and sustain authoritarian regimes through resource-driven geopolitics, highlighting the central role these corporations play in the global crises of inequality, environmental degradation, and autocratic rule.

At the heart of the fossil fuel industry's influence lies a decades-long campaign to deny and obscure the reality of climate change. Since the late 20th century, companies like ExxonMobil, Chevron, and Shell have invested billions of dollars in disinformation efforts aimed at casting doubt on the scientific consensus around climate change. These campaigns mirror the tactics used by the tobacco industry to downplay the health risks of smoking, relying on "think tanks," pseudo-scientific studies, and media manipulation to mislead the public. By funding organizations that deny or minimize the impact of fossil fuel emissions, these companies have delayed meaningful action on climate change, ensuring continued reliance on oil, coal, and gas.

This denial is not merely about protecting profits, it is about maintaining control over global energy systems. Fossil fuel companies understand that transitioning to renewable energy would disrupt their monopolistic grip on the market, shifting power to decentralized systems like wind and solar. To prevent this, they have entrenched themselves in political systems worldwide, using lobbying, campaign donations, and revolving-door politics to influence policymakers. In the United States, for example, fossil fuel lobbyists have worked tirelessly to undermine environmental regulations, block renewable energy initiatives, and protect subsidies that keep oil and gas production artificially cheap.

The influence of fossil fuel companies extends beyond domestic politics to the global stage, where they enable and sustain authoritarian regimes. Many of the world's most repressive governments rely on fossil fuel revenues to maintain power, using resource wealth to fund militarization, suppress dissent, and entrench elite rule. Nations like Saudi Arabia, Russia, and Venezuela are textbook examples of petro-states, countries whose economies and political systems are dominated by fossil fuel production. In these states, oil and gas revenues are used to consolidate authoritarian power, often at the expense of democracy, human rights, and environmental sustainability.

Saudi Arabia, for instance, has long used its vast oil wealth to fund its autocratic monarchy and repress dissent. The kingdom's reliance on fossil fuel exports allows it to maintain a high degree of economic and political control, subsidizing its population to avoid unrest while using its wealth to project influence abroad. The brutal murder of journalist Jamal Khashoggi and the ongoing war in Yemen highlight how Saudi Arabia's oil wealth enables its authoritarian practices and shields it from significant international consequences.

Similarly, Russia's economy is heavily dependent on fossil fuel exports, which account for a substantial portion of its GDP and state budget. Vladimir Putin's regime uses oil and gas revenues to fund its military and security apparatus, suppress domestic opposition, and expand its geopolitical influence. Russia's control over energy supplies has also become a tool of coercion in its foreign policy, particularly in Europe. By leveraging its position as a major supplier of natural gas, Russia has been able to manipulate and divide European nations, undermining collective efforts to address both climate change and Russian aggression.

The fossil fuel industry's role in enabling authoritarian regimes is not limited to resource-rich countries. Multinational energy corporations often collaborate with these regimes to secure access to reserves, turning a blind eye to human rights abuses and environmental degradation. These partnerships reinforce the power of autocratic leaders while ensuring that fossil fuel companies continue to profit from the exploitation of natural resources. This dynamic creates a feedback loop where authoritarian regimes and fossil fuel corporations mutually benefit from the status quo, at the expense of the planet and its people.

The geopolitical implications of this system are profound. Fossil fuel-driven geopolitics perpetuates global inequality, as resource wealth is concentrated in the hands of a few while environmental and social costs are borne by the many. The extraction, transportation, and burning of fossil fuels disproportionately harm marginalized communities, from indigenous groups displaced by oil pipelines to low-income populations suffering from pollution and climate-related disasters. Meanwhile, the wealth generated by fossil fuels rarely benefits the communities where extraction occurs, instead flowing to multinational corporations and corrupt elites.

The fossil fuel industry's grip on global energy systems also undermines international efforts to combat climate change. Despite the growing urgency of the climate crisis, fossil fuel production continues to expand, driven by both corporate and state actors. New oil and gas projects are being developed even as scientists warn that existing reserves must remain unburned to avoid catastrophic warming. This disconnect between scientific reality and industry practices underscores the power of fossil fuel interests to shape policy and public discourse in their favor.

The industry's influence is further amplified by its control over infrastructure and supply chains. Fossil fuel companies have invested heavily in pipelines, refineries, and export terminals, creating physical systems that lock in dependence on oil and gas. These investments are often accompanied by legal agreements and trade deals that prioritize corporate interests over environmental and social concerns. The result is a global energy system that is resistant to change, even as the consequences of inaction become increasingly dire.

The consequences of fossil fuel geopolitics are not limited to climate change, they also contribute to instability and conflict. The competition for control over oil and gas reserves has fueled wars, coups, and territorial disputes, from the U.S. invasion of Iraq to ongoing conflicts in the South China Sea. These resource-driven conflicts are often framed as issues of national security, but they are fundamentally about maintaining access to fossil fuel supplies. The human cost of these conflicts is staggering, with millions displaced, economies destroyed, and countless lives lost in the pursuit of energy dominance.

Meanwhile, the environmental destruction caused by fossil fuel extraction and use exacerbates the climate crisis, creating a feedback loop of harm. Rising temperatures, melting ice caps, and extreme weather events are direct consequences of burning fossil fuels, yet the industry continues to expand, driven by short-term profits rather than long-term sustainability. This destruction disproportionately affects vulnerable populations, who are least responsible for emissions but bear the brunt of their impacts.

The fossil fuel industry's role in perpetuating climate denial and enabling authoritarian regimes is a central obstacle to addressing the climate crisis. Its influence over politics, economics, and public opinion creates a system where meaningful change is not only difficult but actively resisted. To break free from this cycle, the world must confront the power of fossil fuel interests, challenging the systems that prioritize profit over people and the planet. This requires not only reducing reliance on fossil fuels but also addressing the underlying dynamics of inequality, exploitation, and authoritarianism that sustain the industry.

The fight against climate change is not just an environmental issue, it is a struggle for justice, democracy, and the future of humanity. The fossil fuel industry represents one of the greatest barriers to this fight, using its wealth and power to delay action and protect its interests. Yet, as the impacts of the climate crisis become more visible, the need for bold and transformative action grows ever more urgent. The stakes could not be higher.

Environmental Destruction and the Rise of Climate-Based Authoritarian Policies Worldwide

The environmental destruction driven by the fossil fuel industry has not only devastated ecosystems and accelerated climate change but has also created fertile ground for the rise of climate-based authoritarian policies. Around the world, governments are responding to the escalating climate crisis with measures that often prioritize control, suppression, and the consolidation of power over meaningful and equitable solutions. These policies, framed as necessary to address climate-related challenges, mask a deeper agenda: using the crisis as an excuse to erode democratic norms, expand state power, and protect elite interests at the expense of the most vulnerable.

The link between environmental destruction and authoritarianism is clearest in how climate disasters are managed. As rising sea levels, extreme weather events, and resource scarcity become more frequent, governments increasingly invoke emergency powers to maintain order and control. While these powers may be justified in the short term, they are often used to suppress dissent, target marginalized communities, and entrench authoritarian rule. For example, after wildfires and heatwaves devastated parts of India, the government used the chaos as an opportunity to clamp down on environmental activists and NGOs critical of its pro-fossil fuel policies. Similarly, in Brazil, during Jair Bolsonaro's presidency, military forces were deployed to the Amazon under the pretense of fighting illegal deforestation but were instead used to suppress indigenous opposition to resource exploitation.

Climate migration, a direct consequence of environmental destruction, has become another lever of authoritarian control. As millions are displaced by rising seas, droughts, and extreme weather, nations are increasingly militarizing their borders to prevent the flow of climate refugees. This trend is particularly evident in wealthy nations like the United States and the European Union, where harsh immigration policies and border fortifications are justified as necessary responses to "unmanageable" migration. Rather than addressing the root causes of displacement, namely, the continued exploitation of fossil fuels, these policies criminalize the victims of climate change, further marginalizing vulnerable populations and fostering a xenophobic narrative that authoritarian leaders exploit to consolidate power.

The weaponization of climate change is also evident in the rise of green authoritarianism, where governments adopt eco-friendly rhetoric and policies while suppressing dissent and ignoring issues of equity. China's approach to renewable energy exemplifies this trend. While the country has made significant investments in solar, wind, and electric vehicles,

96

these efforts are tightly controlled by the state and accompanied by surveillance, forced labor, and the suppression of activists. The construction of massive renewable energy projects often displaces rural communities, who are given little say in the process. By framing these projects as part of a broader effort to combat climate change, the Chinese government deflects criticism while tightening its grip on power.

In other parts of the world, governments are using climate policies to justify crackdowns on civil liberties and democratic participation. France's "Yellow Vest" protests, which began in response to fuel taxes framed as environmental measures, revealed the dangers of climate policies that prioritize corporate and elite interests over the needs of ordinary people. The French government's heavy-handed response to the protests, including violent police crackdowns, highlighted how environmental measures can be weaponized to silence dissent rather than address systemic inequality. This dynamic is not unique to France; similar patterns are emerging globally as governments seek to manage the political fallout of climate policies that disproportionately affect marginalized communities.

The fossil fuel industry itself plays a role in fostering climate-based authoritarianism. By delaying meaningful action on climate change for decades, fossil fuel companies have created a crisis that demands urgent and often drastic responses. These responses, in turn, create opportunities for governments to expand their power under the guise of managing the crisis. The result is a self-reinforcing cycle: fossil fuel exploitation exacerbates the climate crisis, which then justifies authoritarian measures that protect the very industries responsible for the destruction.

This cycle is particularly evident in regions where resource scarcity is driving conflict and instability. In the Sahel region of Africa, for example, desertification and water shortages, exacerbated by climate change, have fueled violence and displacement. Governments in the region, often backed by international powers, have responded with militarized approaches that do little to address the root causes of the crisis. These policies not only fail to provide sustainable solutions but also entrench authoritarian control, as governments use the pretext of security to suppress opposition and silence critics.

The rise of climate-based authoritarianism also intersects with corporate interests, particularly in the realm of technological solutions. As the climate crisis worsens, tech companies and fossil fuel giants alike are promoting geoengineering and other high-tech fixes as alternatives to systemic change. These solutions, which include carbon capture, solar radiation management, and other speculative technologies, are often framed as silver bullets for the climate crisis. However, they come with significant risks and uncertainties, and their implementation would likely concentrate power in the hands of a few corporations and governments. By prioritizing technological fixes over systemic reform, these actors reinforce existing power structures while delaying the transition to a more equitable and sustainable energy system.

Despite these challenges, resistance to climate-based authoritarianism is growing. Grassroots movements, indigenous activists, and environmental organizations around the world are fighting back against policies that exploit the climate crisis to entrench inequality and authoritarian rule. In the United States, the Sunrise Movement has pushed for a Green New Deal that centers justice and equity, challenging the fossil fuel industry and its political allies. In the Global South, communities are organizing against resource extraction projects that threaten their lands and livelihoods, demanding accountability from both corporations and governments.

One of the most promising aspects of this resistance is its emphasis on intersectionality, recognizing that the fight against climate change is inseparable from struggles for racial justice, economic equality, and human rights. By connecting these issues, activists are building a broader and more inclusive movement that challenges both the root causes of the climate crisis and the systems of power that perpetuate it. This approach offers a powerful counter-narrative to the authoritarian logic that frames the climate crisis as a zero-sum game, where control and suppression are the only solutions.

The rise of climate-based authoritarianism underscores the urgent need for systemic change. Addressing the climate crisis requires more than technical fixes or incremental reforms, it demands a fundamental rethinking of how energy, resources, and power are distributed. This means dismantling the fossil fuel industry's grip on politics and economics, holding corporations accountable for their role in the crisis, and prioritizing policies that center justice, equity, and sustainability.

The stakes could not be higher. The climate crisis is not only an environmental challenge but also a test of humanity's ability to build systems that prioritize collective well-being over individual greed. As the impacts of climate change become increasingly severe, the temptation to respond with authoritarian measures will only grow. Resisting this trend requires vigilance, solidarity, and a commitment to envisioning and fighting for a future that is both just and sustainable. The path forward will not be easy, but it is the only way to ensure that the response to the climate crisis does not deepen the inequalities and injustices that created it.

~10
Media & Propaganda

The Weaponization of State-Controlled Media in Russia, China, and India

State-controlled media has become one of the most potent tools for consolidating power in authoritarian regimes. By controlling the flow of information, regimes in countries like Russia, China, and India have successfully weaponized media to manipulate public opinion, suppress dissent, and entrench their authority. This strategic use of media enables these governments to construct narratives that reinforce their legitimacy while delegitimizing opposition, fostering fear, and sowing division among their populations. In the age of digital communication, where the reach of media is global, these authoritarian tactics not only influence domestic audiences but also shape international perceptions, extending their power far beyond their borders.

In Russia, state-controlled media is the linchpin of Vladimir Putin's authoritarian regime. Through outlets like RT (formerly Russia Today) and Sputnik, the Kremlin has created a media apparatus that operates both domestically and internationally to promote its agenda. Domestically, Russian state media serves as the primary source of information for millions of citizens. It constructs a narrative of Russian nationalism, portraying Putin as a strong leader defending the nation against Western encroachment. Criticism of the regime is framed as unpatriotic, and dissenting voices are labeled as foreign agents or traitors. This narrative is reinforced by a steady stream of propaganda, disinformation, and historical revisionism designed to glorify the state and suppress alternative viewpoints.

Internationally, Russian media operates as a tool of influence and destabilization. RT and Sputnik, funded by the Russian government, target global audiences with content that amplifies divisions within democracies. By spreading disinformation, conspiracy theories, and inflammatory narratives, these outlets aim to undermine trust in democratic institutions and sow discord among political factions. This strategy was particularly evident during the 2016 U.S. presidential election, when Russian media played a key role in amplifying divisive content on social media platforms. By leveraging the openness of democratic societies, the Kremlin has turned state-controlled media into a weapon for weakening its geopolitical adversaries.

China's approach to state-controlled media is equally sophisticated, though it operates within a different framework. The Chinese Communist Party (CCP) maintains an iron grip on domestic media through outlets like Xinhua, CCTV, and the People's Daily. These state-run organizations serve as mouthpieces for the party, delivering tightly controlled narratives that align with its objectives. The CCP's media strategy is built on three pillars: glorifying the party's achievements, suppressing dissent, and projecting China's influence abroad.

Domestically, Chinese state media is a tool of social engineering. It promotes the CCP's vision of a harmonious and prosperous society, emphasizing economic growth, technological advancement, and national unity. At the same time, it suppresses stories that could undermine the party's image, from corruption scandals to environmental disasters. The Chinese government also employs an extensive censorship apparatus, often referred to as the Great Firewall, to control the digital landscape. Social media platforms, search engines, and news websites are tightly monitored, with content that contradicts the party's narrative swiftly removed. This combination of state-controlled media and digital censorship creates an information ecosystem where dissenting voices are virtually nonexistent.

On the international stage, China has expanded its media influence through initiatives like the Belt and Road Initiative (BRI) and partnerships with foreign media outlets. Chinese state media organizations have established bureaus in dozens of countries, broadcasting content that promotes China's vision of global development and its role as a responsible global power. These efforts are complemented by "content-sharing" agreements with foreign media outlets, which often reprint Chinese state media articles uncritically. This strategy allows the CCP to shape global perceptions of China, presenting it as a benign and benevolent force while deflecting criticism of its human rights abuses and authoritarian policies.

India, under the leadership of Narendra Modi and the Bharatiya Janata Party (BJP), has adopted a different but no less effective model of media control. While India's media landscape includes private outlets, many have aligned themselves with the ruling party, either voluntarily or under pressure. The BJP has cultivated a network of loyal media outlets and journalists who propagate its nationalist and Hindu supremacist agenda. Channels like Republic TV and Zee News regularly broadcast content that glorifies Modi, vilifies opposition parties, and stokes communal tensions.

State-controlled media in India works in tandem with corporate-owned outlets that are sympathetic to the BJP. The Modi government has also used its influence over advertising revenue to pressure media organizations into compliance. Outlets that are critical of the government often find themselves targeted through tax raids, regulatory investigations, or the withdrawal of government advertising. This financial pressure, combined with a culture of intimidation and self-censorship, has eroded the independence of India's media landscape.

In all three countries, the weaponization of state-controlled media serves a dual purpose: maintaining domestic control and projecting power internationally. The narratives propagated by these regimes are not only designed to suppress dissent but also to legitimize their authoritarian practices. By controlling the story, these governments ensure that their citizens see them as protectors rather than oppressors. At the same time, they use their media influence to shape global perceptions, presenting themselves as stable, prosperous, and legitimate alternatives to liberal democracies.

The effectiveness of state-controlled media lies in its ability to create echo chambers that reinforce existing biases and suppress critical thinking. In Russia, for example, citizens are bombarded with propaganda that portrays the West as decadent, hypocritical, and hostile to Russian values. This narrative not only justifies the Kremlin's actions but also discourages dissent by framing it as capitulation to foreign influence. Similarly, in China, state media fosters a sense of national pride and unity by emphasizing the country's economic achievements and downplaying its challenges. In India, the BJP's media allies stoke fear of Muslims and other minorities, creating a climate of division that consolidates Hindu nationalist support.

The rise of digital platforms has further amplified the reach and impact of state-controlled media. Social media, in particular, has become a battleground for information warfare, where state narratives compete with independent voices for visibility. Authoritarian regimes have adapted to this new landscape by deploying armies of bots, trolls, and influencers to promote their messages and drown out dissent. In Russia, the Internet Research Agency (IRA) has become infamous for its role in spreading disinformation and manipulating public opinion online. China's "50 Cent Army," a network of government-backed internet commentators, performs a similar function, flooding social media with pro-CCP content and attacking critics. In India, the BJP has leveraged WhatsApp groups and Twitter campaigns to mobilize its base and spread propaganda, often targeting journalists and activists with harassment and threats.

The weaponization of state-controlled media in Russia, China, and India is not just a domestic issue; it has global implications. These regimes are exporting their media models to other countries, offering training, technology, and funding to governments seeking to replicate their success. From Africa to Southeast Asia, authoritarian leaders are adopting tactics pioneered by Moscow, Beijing, and New Delhi to consolidate power and suppress dissent. This trend represents a significant challenge to the global information ecosystem, as the lines between state propaganda, corporate media, and independent journalism continue to blur.

The impact of state-controlled media on democracy cannot be overstated. By monopolizing the narrative, these regimes undermine the very foundations of democratic societies: free speech, an informed citizenry, and accountability. They erode trust in institutions, polarize communities, and create environments where authoritarianism can thrive. The challenge of countering this influence is immense, particularly as state-controlled media adapts to new technologies and platforms.

As the weaponization of media becomes more sophisticated, the need for robust and independent journalism has never been greater. The next part of this chapter will explore the decline of independent journalism in democracies, the role of corporate propaganda in spreading fascist ideologies, and the urgent need for collective action to reclaim the media as a tool for truth and accountability. While the influence of state-controlled media is a formidable challenge, it is not insurmountable. The fight for free and fair information is ultimately a fight for the survival of democracy itself.

The Decline of Independent Journalism in Democracies and the Role of Corporate Propaganda

While state-controlled media serves as a cornerstone of authoritarian regimes, the decline of independent journalism in democracies and the rise of corporate propaganda are equally troubling phenomena. The erosion of journalistic integrity in ostensibly free societies has created fertile ground for the spread of fascist ideologies, allowing governments and corporations to manipulate public discourse with relative ease. This decline is driven by several factors, including the consolidation of media ownership, the financial struggles of traditional news outlets, and the pervasive influence of social media platforms. Together, these forces have hollowed out the Fourth Estate, leaving democracies vulnerable to misinformation, polarization, and authoritarian creep.

The concentration of media ownership is one of the primary drivers of the decline of independent journalism. In countries like the United States, Australia, and the United Kingdom, a handful of conglomerates control the majority of news outlets, creating a homogenized media landscape that prioritizes profit over public interest. Rupert Murdoch's News Corp, for example, owns a significant portion of the global media ecosystem, including Fox News, The Wall Street Journal, The Sun, and numerous other outlets. These organizations often align with conservative political agendas, amplifying narratives that support deregulation, corporate tax cuts, and anti-immigrant policies while marginalizing dissenting voices.

This concentration of ownership stifles diversity in reporting and reduces the media's ability to hold power to account. When news outlets are beholden to corporate interests or shareholders, investigative journalism, often costly and time-consuming, is deprioritized in favor of sensationalist stories that drive clicks and ad revenue. This shift has weakened the media's role as a watchdog, allowing governments and corporations to operate with less scrutiny. At the same time, the consolidation of ownership limits the range of perspectives available to the public, reinforcing dominant narratives and excluding marginalized voices.

106

The financial struggles of traditional news outlets have further exacerbated the decline of independent journalism. The rise of digital media has upended traditional revenue models, with advertising dollars shifting from newspapers and broadcast television to online platforms like Google and Facebook. As a result, many news organizations have been forced to downsize, close bureaus, or shut down entirely. This loss of resources has left gaps in coverage, particularly at the local level, where communities are increasingly underserved by the media. Without robust local reporting, citizens are less informed about the issues that directly affect them, and accountability for local governments and institutions diminishes.

The rise of social media platforms has played a central role in reshaping the media landscape. Platforms like Facebook, Twitter, and YouTube have become primary news sources for millions, but their algorithms prioritize engagement over accuracy. As a result, sensationalist and polarizing content often outperforms balanced, fact-based reporting. This dynamic has created an environment where misinformation spreads rapidly, trust in traditional media erodes, and public discourse fragments. Social media companies have largely escaped accountability for amplifying harmful content, despite mounting evidence of their complicity in spreading conspiracy theories, extremist ideologies, and state-sponsored propaganda.

Corporate propaganda has filled the void left by the decline of independent journalism, leveraging the reach and influence of modern media to shape public opinion in ways that benefit the wealthy and powerful. This propaganda often takes the form of advertorials, sponsored content, or "native advertising" that blurs the line between journalism and corporate messaging. Energy companies, for example, have spent billions on campaigns that greenwash their image, presenting themselves as champions of sustainability while continuing to extract and burn fossil fuels. These campaigns are carefully designed to mislead the public, creating the illusion of corporate responsibility while delaying meaningful action on climate change.

The influence of corporate propaganda extends beyond advertising to the editorial decisions of media outlets. News organizations that rely on advertising revenue from industries like fossil fuels, pharmaceuticals, or defense may be reluctant to publish stories that criticize those industries. This self-censorship, whether explicit or implicit, creates a media environment where certain topics are underreported or framed in ways that align with corporate interests. The result is a skewed understanding of critical issues, from climate change to healthcare, that serves the status quo rather than the public good.

The decline of independent journalism and the rise of corporate propaganda have had profound implications for democracy. Without a robust and independent media, citizens lack the information needed to make informed decisions, hold leaders accountable, and participate meaningfully in public life. The erosion of trust in traditional media, fueled by both genuine failures and deliberate attacks from authoritarian leaders, has further undermined democratic norms. When citizens cannot agree on a shared set of facts, the foundation of democracy begins to crumble, leaving a vacuum that authoritarian forces are all too eager to fill.

In this environment, fascist ideologies find fertile ground. The decline of independent journalism creates space for disinformation and propaganda that reinforce authoritarian narratives. In the United States, for example, right-wing media ecosystems have played a central role in normalizing extremism, amplifying conspiracy theories like QAnon, and undermining trust in democratic institutions. Similar trends can be seen in countries like Brazil, where Bolsonaro leveraged social media and right-leaning outlets to spread misinformation about COVID-19, elections, and his political opponents. These examples highlight how the weakening of the Fourth Estate enables the rise of fascism, as unchecked power thrives in the absence of accountability.

Despite these challenges, there are signs of hope. Independent journalism, though embattled, continues to play a vital role in exposing corruption, challenging propaganda, and amplifying marginalized voices. Investigative reporting on issues like systemic racism, corporate malfeasance, and climate change has sparked public debate and driven meaningful change. Nonprofit journalism organizations, such as ProPublica and The Intercept, are stepping in to fill the gaps left by traditional outlets, demonstrating the resilience and adaptability of the media in the face of adversity.

Efforts to counter corporate propaganda and state-controlled media are gaining momentum. Media literacy initiatives aim to equip citizens with tools to critically evaluate information, while advocacy groups push for stronger regulations on advertising and media ownership. Simultaneously, grassroots movements leverage digital platforms to bypass traditional gatekeepers, creating alternative channels for sharing information and organizing action.

The fight for independent journalism and truthful media is inseparable from the broader struggle for democracy and human rights. As authoritarian regimes and corporate interests weaponize media to consolidate power, the need for a free and fair press has never been more urgent. Without independent journalism, democracy cannot survive. With effort, creativity, and commitment to the public good, we can reclaim media as a force for accountability, justice, and truth. The challenge is immense, but the stakes demand nothing less than full attention and action.

Finance & The Greed Virus

The Pathology of Billionaires—How Sociopathy, Hoarding, and Evil Perpetuate Authoritarianism

The global financial system has become a playground for the ultra-wealthy, where billionaires operate above the rules that govern ordinary citizens. These individuals do not simply embody greed, they exhibit a pathological hoarding of resources and power that undermines democracy, entrenches inequality, and sustains fascist control over governments and industries. Studies have increasingly shown that many billionaires exhibit traits associated with sociopathy, including a lack of empathy, manipulative tendencies, and an insatiable need for control. This isn't just about flawed systems; it's about the individuals who drive them, a small cadre of people who might just meet the definition of evil, perpetuating harm on a global scale.

At the core of this pathology is the staggering concentration of wealth in the hands of a few. Billionaires hoard resources not merely to maintain their lifestyles but to exert disproportionate influence over political and economic systems. Hoarding is recognized as a psychological disorder, yet in the financial realm, it is celebrated as success. These individuals lock their wealth in investments, trusts, and tax havens, ensuring its exponential growth while depriving society of the resources needed to address systemic challenges like poverty, healthcare, and climate change. The result is a feedback loop where their insatiable greed begets more power, which they use to further manipulate the systems that protect their wealth.

The use of tax havens exemplifies this pathological behavior. By exploiting loopholes in international tax laws, billionaires funnel trillions of dollars into offshore accounts in jurisdictions like the Cayman Islands, Luxembourg, and Switzerland.

These havens offer secrecy, low or no tax rates, and protection from scrutiny, enabling the wealthy to avoid contributing to the societies they profit from. Meanwhile, ordinary citizens are burdened with rising taxes and austerity measures, forced to make up for the shortfall created by these hoarders. The Pandora Papers and similar investigations have revealed the extent of this practice, yet the scale of inaction suggests these individuals operate not only outside the law but outside basic moral considerations.

The pathology extends beyond wealth hoarding to active harm. Many billionaires fund authoritarian regimes, sustaining systems that oppress millions while enriching a small elite. Russian oligarchs, for instance, amassed their fortunes during the post-Soviet privatization of state assets and became loyal allies of Vladimir Putin. In exchange for their loyalty, they enjoy significant influence over industries and access to lucrative state contracts, creating a symbiotic relationship that reinforces authoritarian control. These oligarchs are not passive beneficiaries of the system, they are active participants in perpetuating its abuses, manipulating power structures to entrench their dominance.

The same dynamics are at play in nations like Saudi Arabia, where fossil fuel wealth funds one of the most repressive regimes on the planet. The Saudi royal family's investments in Western corporations and luxury assets serve to whitewash their image while enabling the suppression of dissent and brutal human rights abuses. Billionaires and corporations eagerly engage with such regimes, reaping profits while ignoring the suffering of those crushed under authoritarian rule. This willingness to prioritize profit over humanity reflects the moral vacuum at the heart of the billionaire class, a vacuum that might well be described as demonic.

Studies have shown that the ultra-wealthy often score higher on scales measuring traits like narcissism, psychopathy, and Machiavellianism. These traits align disturbingly well with the

112

behaviors observed in billionaires: the manipulation of systems for personal gain, the exploitation of labor, and the callous disregard for the lives affected by their actions. It's no exaggeration to say that many of these individuals meet the clinical definition of sociopathy. Their inability, or refusal, to empathize with those harmed by their wealth accumulation makes them uniquely dangerous in positions of power. When sociopathic tendencies are paired with immense resources, the result is a system that prioritizes the desires of the few over the needs of the many.

This sociopathy manifests not only in their personal behavior but in the systems they create and sustain. Billionaires have funded far-right movements, think tanks, and political campaigns that undermine democracy and promote authoritarianism. In the United States, figures like the Koch brothers (and their network) have poured billions into efforts to attack voting rights, dismantle environmental protections, and weaken labor unions. These campaigns are not merely ideological, they are calculated attempts to entrench the power of the wealthy while eroding the rights of ordinary people.

The hoarding and manipulation of wealth by billionaires also have a spiritual dimension that cannot be ignored. The harm they cause, whether through environmental destruction, the exploitation of workers, or the funding of authoritarian regimes, raises the question of whether these individuals embody something far darker than simple greed. Across cultures and religions, the concept of evil is often tied to the deliberate infliction of harm and the prioritization of selfish desires over the collective good. By this measure, the actions of many billionaires may indeed be described as evil. Their disregard for the suffering they cause, coupled with their relentless pursuit of wealth, suggests a level of moral corruption that borders on the demonic.

The global impact of this pathology is staggering. Billionaires and their financial practices perpetuate cycles of inequality, environmental degradation, and political instability. Their hoarding of resources deprives governments of the funds needed to address crises like climate change, while their influence over political systems ensures that policies favor their interests over those of the broader population. This dynamic creates a world where the rich grow richer, the poor are left behind, and authoritarian regimes thrive under the financial and ideological support of the ultra-wealthy.

Addressing this pathology requires more than incremental reforms, it demands a fundamental shift in how society views and manages wealth and power. The concentration of wealth in the hands of a few is not just an economic issue; it is a moral crisis that threatens the stability of democracies and the future of the planet. Billionaires are not benevolent figures to be admired; they are hoarders of resources, enablers of authoritarianism, and architects of systems that prioritize their greed over the collective good.

To confront the greed virus, and the sociopathy that fuels it, society must rewrite the rules of global finance. This includes implementing wealth taxes, closing tax haven loopholes, and creating systems of accountability that hold billionaires responsible for the harm they cause. It also means challenging the cultural narratives that glorify extreme wealth and reframing success in terms of community well-being rather than individual accumulation. Only by addressing the pathological behaviors of the ultra-wealthy can humanity begin to dismantle the systems of inequality and oppression that sustain them.

The greed virus is not inevitable, nor is it insurmountable. It thrives in a system designed to reward selfishness and punish equity, but systems can be changed. The fight against this pathology is a fight for justice, democracy, and the survival of the planet. It is a fight to reclaim humanity from the clutches of those who have traded empathy and morality for the false promise of limitless wealth. The stakes are too high to allow this sociopathy to go unchecked. If billionaires are the architects of modern greed, then it is time to dismantle their edifices and rebuild a world where the many matter more than the few.

The Greed Virus: The Myth of Meritocracy, Class Warfare, and Gaslighting in the Age of Billionaire Domination

The billionaire class thrives on myths and manipulations that sustain its grip on global power. Chief among these is the myth of meritocracy, the idea that their immense wealth and influence are the result of hard work and innovation. This narrative, repeated in media and politics, paints billionaires as deserving winners in a system that rewards talent. Yet the reality is far different. The American Dream, which claims anyone can rise through determination, is statistically dead. Billionaire wealth is not earned in a vacuum but built on systems of exploitation, rigged policies, and redistribution of wealth from the bottom to the top.

The myth of meritocracy serves as a smokescreen to justify inequality. Billionaires use this narrative to deflect criticism, framing challenges to their wealth as attacks on ambition. What they fail to mention is how fortunes often stem from inherited wealth, insider connections, and market manipulation. Studies show many billionaires were born into privilege, benefiting from elite education and networks most will never access. For all their "bootstrap" rhetoric, billionaires are often beneficiaries of a system designed to keep them on top.

This system represents "socialism for the rich and rugged individualism for the poor," as FDR described. Billionaires use wealth to lobby for tax cuts, subsidies, and bailouts that keep their empires intact, even during crises. Meanwhile, working-class people are told to endure stagnant wages and shoulder healthcare, education, and housing costs. The 2008 financial crisis epitomized this: billionaires got bailouts while ordinary people lost homes, savings, and jobs.

This redistribution of wealth upward isn't accidental; it is deliberate class warfare. Decades of tax cuts for the wealthy, from Reaganomics to Trump's 2017 tax overhaul, shifted the public service funding burden onto the middle class. Loopholes and offshore accounts allow billionaires to pay little to no taxes, resulting in a system where the richest pay less than teachers and nurses. This isn't free-market capitalism; it's a rigged game, designed by and for the ultra-wealthy. The billionaire class has also weaponized division as a strategy to maintain their power. By fueling the left-right political divide, they distract the public from the real source of inequality: their own hoarding of resources and manipulation of the system. Cultural wedge issues, whether it's immigration, abortion, or gun rights, are amplified by media empires like Rupert Murdoch's, keeping people focused on ideological battles while billionaires quietly rewrite the tax code and dismantle worker protections. This deliberate division ensures that the public fights among themselves instead of uniting against the true architects of inequality.

Gaslighting is a key tool in this strategy. Billionaires and their allies consistently frame class warfare as a fiction, accusing critics of promoting envy or socialism. They portray themselves as benevolent job creators, conveniently ignoring how their companies exploit workers, suppress wages, and offshore jobs to maximize profits. This narrative is reinforced through philanthropy, where billionaires donate a fraction of their wealth to high-profile causes to distract from the systemic harm they cause. The result is a public perception that billionaires are generous benefactors rather than the architects of inequality.

This gaslighting extends to the very language of economics. Phrases like "trickle-down economics" and "the free market" are used to mask policies that overwhelmingly benefit the rich. The idea that wealth will naturally flow from the top to the bottom has been debunked time and again, yet it remains a central tenet of economic policy in many countries. In reality, wealth flows in the opposite direction, as billionaires extract resources, exploit labor, and avoid taxes, all while blaming government regulations or market inefficiencies for the struggles of ordinary people.

The impact of this billionaire-driven class war is evident in the erosion of social mobility and the widening wealth gap. In the United States, the richest 1% now control more wealth than the bottom 90% combined. The so-called American Dream, a promise of upward mobility through hard work, has become a cruel joke for most Americans, as the barriers to success grow ever higher. Education, once a pathway to opportunity, has become a crushing financial burden for millions, while affordable housing is increasingly out of reach for working families. These systemic failures are not accidents; they are the inevitable result of policies designed to protect and expand the wealth of the billionaire class.

Internationally, this class war plays out in even starker terms. In the Global South, billions of people live in poverty while multinational corporations extract resources, exploit labor, and evade taxes. The wealth generated by these practices flows to the Global North, enriching billionaires and perpetuating cycles of inequality. At the same time, developing nations are burdened with debt and forced to implement austerity measures that further impoverish their populations. This global redistribution of wealth is not just a moral failure; it is a form of neocolonialism that ensures the dominance of the ultra-wealthy at the expense of billions.

Addressing this system of inequality requires more than exposing its mechanics; it demands collective action to dismantle the structures that sustain it. This begins with rejecting the myths that justify billionaire domination, the myth of meritocracy, the myth of trickle-down economics, and the myth that billionaires are job creators. It also means challenging the language of division and recognizing that the real battle is not between left and right but between the many and the few. This is not a class war started by workers or progressives, it is a war declared and waged by billionaires, and they have been winning for decades.

Reclaiming power from the billionaire class will require bold, systemic changes. This includes implementing wealth taxes, closing tax haven loopholes, and creating global frameworks to hold billionaires accountable for their exploitation and evasion. It also means investing in public goods like education, healthcare, and infrastructure, funded by those who have profited most from society. But perhaps most importantly, it requires a cultural shift, a rejection of the narrative that extreme wealth is a sign of success and an embrace of the idea that collective well-being is the true measure of progress.

The billionaire class has built an empire on lies, manipulation, and exploitation, but their power is not invincible. It thrives on division, apathy, and the belief that change is impossible. This is all endemic of the greed virus, a pathological system that prioritizes wealth and power for the few at the expense of humanity and the planet. Yet history has shown that systems of inequality can be dismantled when people unite to demand justice. The fight against the greed virus and the sociopathy of the billionaire class is not just an economic struggle, it is a fight for the soul of humanity. The time to act is now, before their pathology leads us further into environmental collapse, authoritarian control, and the death of democracy itself. We must choose collective action over despair and transformation over destruction, for our survival depends on it.

Special Note: Fintech, Bitcoin, and the Promise of Decentralization

The rise of fintech and cryptocurrencies promised a revolution in finance, but the reality has been far more complicated. Bitcoin, as the pioneer of decentralized digital currency, has its merits, offering transparency, resistance to inflationary manipulation, and freedom from centralized control. However, the ecosystem surrounding Bitcoin has become rife with scams, and the proliferation of "shitcoins," unregulated, speculative cryptocurrencies, has turned much of the industry into a breeding ground for greed and exploitation. Even Bitcoin itself is surrounded by dubious actors and fraudulent schemes, eroding public trust in its original purpose.

The solution is not more of the same speculative chaos but robust education and critical thinking about what decentralization can truly achieve. Blockchain and smart contracts hold immense potential for creating transparent, accountable systems that reduce reliance on corruptible intermediaries. However, their value lies in their ability to operate independently of human greed. To realize this potential, these technologies must be designed to be immune to manipulation, ensuring that the "greed virus" doesn't infect decentralized systems as it has traditional ones.

Decentralized finance (DeFi) can democratize access to economic opportunities, but only if implemented with clear safeguards and accountability. Moving forward, the focus must shift from speculative gains to building systems that prioritize equity, sustainability, and resilience. The promise of blockchain is too important to waste on scams and greed. Education and thoughtful development are the keys to unlocking a future where technology serves humanity, not the other way around.

~12

Pharma & Health 'Care'

Vaccine Apartheid, Inequitable Healthcare Systems, and the Weaponization of Public Health Crises

The COVID-19 pandemic laid bare the fault lines of global healthcare inequity, exposing a world where access to life-saving medicines and vaccines is determined not by need but by wealth, power, and geography. Vaccine apartheid, the stark disparity in vaccine availability between wealthy and low-income nations, became a defining feature of the pandemic response. While developed countries hoarded vaccines, securing multiple doses per citizen, much of the Global South struggled to obtain even a fraction of the doses needed. This injustice is not an anomaly; it is the logical outcome of a healthcare system dominated by profit-driven pharmaceutical companies, complicit governments, and the entrenched inequality that defines the modern world.

Vaccine apartheid is perhaps the clearest example of how healthcare systems reflect broader social and economic disparities. Countries like the United States and members of the European Union were able to leverage their wealth and political influence to secure early access to COVID-19 vaccines, often pre-purchasing billions of doses before clinical trials were even complete. Meanwhile, low-income nations were left to rely on international aid programs like COVAX, which, while well-intentioned, were woefully underfunded and poorly managed. This disparity in vaccine distribution had devastating consequences. While wealthy nations debated booster shots, healthcare workers and vulnerable populations in poorer countries went unvaccinated, leading to preventable deaths and the proliferation of new variants.

This imbalance is rooted in the structure of the pharmaceutical industry, which prioritizes profit over public health. Vaccine development and distribution are controlled by a handful of multinational corporations like Pfizer, Moderna, and AstraZeneca, which hold patents on their products and tightly control their production. These patents, often developed with substantial public funding, grant pharmaceutical companies monopolies that allow them to set exorbitant prices and restrict supply. Calls to waive these patents during the pandemic to allow generic production were met with fierce resistance, as companies argued that such measures would undermine innovation. In reality, this resistance was about protecting profit margins, even at the cost of human lives.

Authoritarian regimes have exploited these inequities to further their own agendas, weaponizing public health crises to consolidate power and suppress dissent. In countries like China and Russia, state-controlled vaccine production became a tool of geopolitical influence, with vaccines used as bargaining chips in diplomatic negotiations. Domestically, these regimes framed their vaccine rollouts as evidence of their superiority, while cracking down on dissent and controlling narratives about their pandemic responses. In China, the government used the pandemic as an opportunity to expand its surveillance apparatus, implementing digital health codes that track citizens' movements and restrict access to public spaces based on vaccination status. While these measures were framed as necessary for public health, they also served to tighten the state's control over its population.

The weaponization of public health crises is not limited to authoritarian regimes; even democracies have used the pandemic as a pretext to expand state power and suppress opposition. In India, the government of Narendra Modi exploited the crisis to crack down on protests, silence critics, and centralize authority. The distribution of vaccines and medical supplies was heavily politicized, with opposition-led states receiving fewer resources. This selective allocation of aid underscored how public health crises can be manipulated to entrench power, exacerbating existing inequalities and deepening social divisions.

Inequitable healthcare systems are not unique to global disparities; they are mirrored within nations as well. In the United States, the pandemic highlighted the systemic racism and classism embedded in the healthcare system. Black and Brown communities, already disproportionately burdened by chronic illnesses due to structural inequities, suffered higher infection and mortality rates. These disparities were compounded by unequal access to testing, treatment, and vaccines, reflecting a healthcare system that prioritizes those who can pay over those who are most in need. Essential workers, often low-wage employees from marginalized communities, were lauded as heroes while being denied basic protections and access to healthcare, underscoring the hypocrisy of a system that exploits labor while failing to safeguard lives.

The privatization of healthcare is a central driver of these inequities. In the United States and other nations with privatized systems, healthcare is treated as a commodity rather than a human right. Insurance companies, hospital chains, and pharmaceutical corporations prioritize profits over patient outcomes, creating barriers to access that disproportionately affect the poor and marginalized. The result is a two-tiered system where the wealthy receive high-quality care, while the uninsured and underinsured are left to navigate underfunded public systems or forego care entirely. This privatized model not only perpetuates inequality but also undermines public health by creating gaps in care that allow preventable diseases to spread.

Globally, the privatization of medicine has entrenched class and racial disparities, as wealthy nations and corporations dominate the development, production, and distribution of life-saving treatments. Pharmaceutical companies focus their research on diseases that affect affluent markets, neglecting conditions like malaria and tuberculosis that primarily impact the Global South. Even when treatments for these diseases exist, they are often priced out of reach for the populations that need them most. This prioritization of profit over public health is not just a moral failing; it is a systemic flaw that perpetuates cycles of poverty, illness, and inequality.

The pandemic also exposed the fragility of healthcare systems in the face of global crises. Even in wealthy nations, hospitals were overwhelmed, supply chains collapsed, and healthcare workers were pushed to the brink. These failures were not inevitable but the result of decades of austerity, underfunding, and privatization that prioritized efficiency over resilience. The lack of investment in public health infrastructure left nations ill-prepared to respond to a pandemic, forcing governments to improvise and leaving vulnerable populations to bear the brunt of the consequences.

The concept of vaccine apartheid extends beyond COVID-19, reflecting a broader pattern of inequitable access to healthcare that affects everything from cancer treatments to maternal health. The same dynamics that allowed wealthy nations to hoard vaccines during the pandemic also drive disparities in access to essential medicines, medical technologies, and preventive care. These inequities are not accidents but the outcomes of deliberate choices made by governments, corporations, and international institutions to prioritize profit and power over human lives.

Addressing these disparities requires systemic change that goes beyond addressing individual crises. It demands a reimagining of healthcare as a universal right rather than a privilege reserved for the wealthy. This includes challenging the monopolies of pharmaceutical companies, investing in public health infrastructure, and creating mechanisms to ensure equitable access to life-saving treatments. It also requires addressing the root causes of health inequities, including systemic racism, economic inequality, and the exploitation of labor.

The inequities in global healthcare systems are a reflection of the broader structures of power and inequality that define our world. Vaccine apartheid, privatization, and the weaponization of public health crises are not isolated issues; they are symptoms of a system that prioritizes the interests of the few over the needs of the many. Confronting these inequities is not just a matter of justice, it is a matter of survival, as the interconnectedness of global health means that no one is safe until everyone is.

The greed virus that permeates healthcare systems, prioritizing profits over lives, must be dismantled. The fight for equitable healthcare is inseparable from the fight for a more just and sustainable world. Only by addressing the structural flaws in our systems can we hope to create a future where healthcare is not a privilege but a fundamental human right. The next part of this chapter will explore how the privatization of medicine and economic inequities reinforce these disparities, and what it will take to dismantle these systems of oppression.

The Privatization of Medicine and How Economic Inequities Reinforce Class and Racial Disparities

The privatization of medicine has entrenched class and racial disparities within healthcare systems worldwide, creating a structure that rewards wealth and punishes vulnerability. By treating healthcare as a commodity rather than a human right, the privatized model has systematically prioritized profits over patients, exacerbating inequities that are deeply rooted in economic and social hierarchies. This profit-driven system not only determines who receives care but also shapes the quality, accessibility, and affordability of that care, ensuring that those with the least resources bear the greatest burden.

In the United States, the privatization of healthcare is glaring. For-profit insurance companies act as gatekeepers to medical access, determining who can afford care. Even those with insurance face crippling medical bills, high deductibles, and limited coverage. The privatized system forces patients to make impossible choices between health and financial stability, leaving millions uninsured or underinsured. Meanwhile, pharmaceutical companies charge astronomical prices for essential medications, from insulin to cancer treatments, driving many into debt or forcing them to forego life-saving treatments. These dynamics disproportionately impact low-income communities and communities of color, reinforcing cycles of poverty and illness.

The racial disparities within privatized healthcare systems are stark. Black and Brown Americans are more likely to lack insurance, less likely to receive preventive care, and more likely to suffer from untreated chronic illnesses. These disparities reflect the intersection of systemic racism and economic inequality. Hospitals in predominantly Black and Brown communities are often underfunded, understaffed, and ill-equipped, while wealthier, predominantly white areas enjoy access to state-of-the-art facilities. This geographic segregation of healthcare access mirrors broader patterns of economic and racial inequality, ensuring marginalized communities bear the brunt of the system's failures.

Globally, the privatization of medicine has created similar patterns of exclusion and inequity. Pharmaceutical companies dominate the development, production, and distribution of medications, prioritizing diseases that affect wealthy markets while neglecting those that disproportionately impact the Global South. Conditions like malaria, tuberculosis, and HIV/AIDS, which primarily affect low-income countries, receive far less investment in research and development compared to diseases prevalent in affluent nations. Even when treatments for these diseases exist, they are often priced out of reach for the populations that need them most. This neglect is

126

a stark reminder that in a privatized system, human lives are valued not by their intrinsic worth but by their market potential.

Economic inequities within healthcare are further reinforced by the commodification of medical education and training. The rising cost of medical school deters students from low-income backgrounds, perpetuating a lack of diversity within the healthcare workforce. This lack of representation has tangible consequences, as studies show that patients often receive better care from providers who share their cultural or linguistic background. The privatized model thus not only determines who can access care but also who can provide it, ensuring that economic inequality permeates every level of the system.

The privatization of medicine has also created a global marketplace where healthcare is treated as a luxury good, accessible only to those who can afford it. Medical tourism, for example, has become a booming industry, with wealthy patients traveling to other countries for specialized treatments while local populations struggle to access basic care. This dynamic reinforces global inequities, as resources are diverted to cater to affluent foreigners rather than addressing the needs of local communities. The result is a healthcare system that prioritizes profit over equity, leaving millions without access to the care they need.

Authoritarian regimes have exploited the privatization of medicine to further entrench their power, using access to healthcare as a tool of control. In countries like Venezuela, the government has manipulated the distribution of medical supplies and services to reward loyalty and punish dissent. Public hospitals are chronically underfunded, while private clinics cater to the wealthy and politically connected. This dual system creates a stark divide between those who have access to care and those who do not, reinforcing existing inequalities and deepening societal divisions.

The weaponization of healthcare is not limited to authoritarian regimes; even democracies have used access to medical care as a means of control. During the COVID-19 pandemic, governments and corporations alike used vaccine distribution as leverage, prioritizing political allies and wealthy nations while marginalizing the Global South. This dynamic reflects a broader trend within privatized healthcare systems, where access to life-saving treatments is determined not by need but by wealth and influence. The result is a system that perpetuates global inequality, with devastating consequences for the most vulnerable populations.

The privatization of healthcare also exacerbates the global brain drain, as skilled medical professionals from low-income countries are lured to wealthier nations by higher salaries and better working conditions. This migration leaves poorer countries with severe shortages of doctors, nurses, and other healthcare workers, further weakening their healthcare systems. Wealthy nations benefit from this influx of talent while failing to address the root causes of the disparities that drive migration in the first place. This dynamic is yet another example of how privatized medicine reinforces global inequities, prioritizing the needs of affluent nations over those of the Global South.

Addressing the failures of privatized medicine requires systemic change that challenges the profit-driven logic at the heart of the system. This begins with recognizing healthcare as a fundamental human right, rather than a commodity to be bought and sold. Universal healthcare systems, like those in Canada and much of Europe, provide models for how care can be delivered equitably and sustainably. These systems prioritize public funding, preventive care, and accessible services, ensuring that healthcare is available to all, regardless of income or status.

However, implementing such systems on a global scale requires more than policy changes; it demands a cultural shift that prioritizes collective well-being over individual profit.

128

Pharmaceutical companies must be held accountable for perpetuating inequities, from price gouging to neglecting diseases that primarily affect low-income populations. This includes breaking up monopolies, reforming patent laws, and incentivizing research into neglected diseases. At the same time, governments must invest in public health infrastructure to ensure healthcare systems are resilient, equitable, and prepared to address future crises.

Efforts to address economic inequities in healthcare must confront the broader systems of power and privilege that sustain them. This includes tackling systemic racism, addressing income inequality, and ensuring marginalized communities have a voice in shaping policies. Representation within the healthcare workforce must be prioritized, with efforts to support students from underrepresented backgrounds. These changes are essential for achieving equity and rebuilding trust in systems that have failed the vulnerable.

The privatization of medicine and its inequities result from deliberate choices by governments, corporations, and institutions. Reversing these trends requires a collective commitment to reimagine healthcare as a public good rather than a private commodity. This is not just a moral imperative, it is a necessity, as global health's interconnectedness means no one is safe until everyone is.

The greed driving healthcare privatization must be confronted. This is not just a fight for healthcare; it is a fight for justice, equity, and humanity's future. By dismantling systems of inequality and exploitation, we can create a world where healthcare is a right for all, not a privilege for the few. The stakes could not be higher, but the path forward is clear: prioritize people over profit and reclaim healthcare as the foundation of a just society.

Section 3
Revolution – Fighting Back

~13
Building the Rising TIDE

Targeting the Key Players and Institutions

The Rising TIDE strategy—Target, Inspire, Disrupt, Empower—offers a clear roadmap for dismantling the deeply entrenched systems of greed and inequality that dominate our world. This strategy begins with identifying and targeting the key players and institutions that actively perpetuate harm. These are not passive beneficiaries of a broken system; they are its architects and enablers, individuals and entities that have used their wealth, influence, and power to exploit humanity and the planet for their own gain.

To understand the scale of their influence, consider the corporate oligarchs who control vast swaths of global resources, the complicit politicians who have sold out their constituents to serve these elites, and the global institutions that protect the interests of the few at the expense of the many. These players are not just part of the problem, they *are* the problem. They have rigged the system to ensure their continued dominance, wielding their power to suppress opposition, consolidate wealth, and dismantle protections for the vulnerable.

Corporate Oligarchs: The Cornerstone of Greed

Corporate oligarchs sit at the pinnacle of this hierarchy, using their wealth to dictate policies, manipulate markets, and erode democratic safeguards. These are the billionaires and

multinational corporations that thrive on exploitation, from
fossil fuel giants that accelerate climate change to tech
monopolies that harvest and weaponize our data. They
operate behind a facade of innovation and philanthropy, but
their true motives are clear: profit at any cost, regardless of the
human or environmental toll.

Targeting corporate oligarchs requires shining a light on their
practices and holding them accountable. These entities thrive
on public complacency and a lack of scrutiny, relying on the
complexity of their operations to evade responsibility. The first
step in dismantling their influence is exposure. Investigative
journalism, whistleblowing, and public awareness campaigns
are critical tools for revealing the extent of their exploitation.
Once exposed, action must follow, boycotts to hit their profits,
divestment campaigns to undermine their financial stability,
and public shaming to damage their carefully curated
reputations.

Complicit Politicians: The Gatekeepers of Corruption

If corporate oligarchs are the architects of systemic greed,
complicit politicians are its gatekeepers. These elected officials
have abandoned their duty to represent the people, choosing
instead to serve as enablers of the wealthy and powerful. They
pass laws that protect corporations from accountability,
defund social programs that support the vulnerable, and use
their platforms to sow division and deflect attention from the
true sources of inequality.

The Rising TIDE strategy demands a fundamental shift in
how we view these politicians. They are not allies in the fight
for justice; they are barriers to progress. Meeting with them,
pleading for action, or expecting them to prioritize the public
good is a waste of time and energy. The system that produced
these politicians is designed to ensure their loyalty to donors
and elites, not to the people they claim to serve. It is time to
132

stop legitimizing their authority and focus instead on building systems that bypass their influence entirely.

Grassroots movements must reject the legitimacy of complicit politicians and work to dismantle the structures that empower them. This includes exposing their ties to corporate interests, holding them accountable for their actions, and creating alternatives to the systems they represent. Technology offers new tools for achieving this, enabling communities to organize, communicate, and govern themselves without reliance on traditional political institutions.

Global Elites: The Protectors of the Status Quo

Beyond corporate oligarchs and politicians, there exists a global network of elites who operate in the shadows, shaping policies and influencing decisions on a scale that defies accountability. These include international financial institutions, think tanks, and organizations that claim to work for the global good but often prioritize the interests of the wealthy and powerful. They perpetuate a global system of inequality, where the Global South is exploited for resources, labor, and markets while the Global North reaps the benefits.

Targeting these elites requires disrupting the systems that protect them. This includes challenging trade agreements that prioritize corporate profits over human rights, exposing the influence of lobbying groups that dictate policy, and mobilizing international opposition to hold them accountable. The Rising TIDE strategy emphasizes the need to act globally while thinking locally, recognizing that the fight against systemic greed transcends borders.

Actionable Steps for Targeting Key Players

The Rising TIDE strategy provides a framework for taking action against these enablers of systemic greed. Here are some key steps:

1.   Expose and Educate: Raise public awareness of the actions and influence of corporate oligarchs, politicians, and global elites. Use investigative journalism, whistleblowing, and social media to share information widely.

2.   Boycott and Divest: Hit these players where it hurts, their bottom line. Organize boycotts of exploitative companies and push for divestment from industries that harm people and the planet.

3.   Public Shaming: Damage their reputations through coordinated campaigns that highlight their greed, corruption, and exploitation. Use storytelling and social media to make their actions visible and unacceptable.

4.   Legal Challenges: Support lawsuits and legal actions against corporations and politicians that violate laws or harm communities. Use the courts to hold them accountable and set precedents for future cases.

5.   Build Alternatives: Create community-led systems that bypass traditional power structures. Use technology to empower individuals and groups to govern themselves and meet their own needs.

Why They Are Not Allies

It is crucial to recognize that these individuals and institutions are not allies in the fight for justice. They have built their wealth and power on the exploitation of others and have no incentive to dismantle the systems that sustain them. Expecting them to act in the public interest is not only naive but counterproductive. The Rising TIDE strategy rejects the idea that change can come from within these systems. Instead, it focuses on building opposition movements that challenge their legitimacy and create new models of governance and accountability.

By targeting these key players and institutions, the Rising TIDE strategy aims to dismantle the foundations of systemic greed and corruption. This is not a task that can be accomplished overnight, but it is an essential step toward reclaiming power and building a future that prioritizes equity, justice, and sustainability. The fight is not abstract, it is against real people and institutions who have chosen greed over humanity. The Rising TIDE is a call to action to hold them accountable and create the conditions for lasting change.

Inspiring and Empowering Grassroots Movements

The Rising TIDE strategy is not just about targeting the powerful, it's about empowering the many. Grassroots movements are the backbone of systemic change. They represent the collective will of ordinary people rising against extraordinary injustices, often succeeding where governments and institutions fail. Decentralized, adaptive, and resilient, grassroots movements have the potential to disrupt entrenched systems of greed and build alternatives that prioritize equity, justice, and sustainability.

The Role of Grassroots Movements in the Rising TIDE

History is full of examples where grassroots organizing has been the driving force behind transformative change. From civil rights movements to environmental activism, change is rarely initiated from the top down. Instead, it begins with communities recognizing their shared struggles and organizing to confront systemic injustices. The Rising TIDE strategy seeks to harness this power by inspiring and equipping grassroots movements to act as catalysts for a larger transformation.

In a world where governments are increasingly beholden to corporate interests, grassroots movements provide an alternative path to reclaim power. They bypass traditional political institutions, focusing instead on direct action and community-driven solutions. By rejecting the authority of complicit politicians and elites, grassroots organizers shift the focus to what matters: meeting the needs of the people, holding the powerful accountable, and building systems that serve the many rather than the few.

Rejecting Traditional Power Structures

One of the most important lessons of the Rising TIDE strategy is that we can no longer rely on traditional power structures to enact change. Politicians, even those who claim to represent the people, have repeatedly shown their loyalty lies with donors and elites. Meeting with local "electeds" to beg for action or expecting them to prioritize public good is not only futile, it's counterproductive. The system that produces these politicians is designed to maintain the status quo, and working within it only reinforces its legitimacy.

Grassroots movements, by contrast, operate outside these structures. They create alternative systems of governance, mutual aid, and accountability that are more democratic and responsive to the needs of their communities. Technology has made it easier than ever to organize, communicate, and build these alternatives, offering tools that empower individuals and groups to bypass traditional gatekeepers and take direct action.

The Power of Decentralization

Decentralization is one of the greatest strengths of grassroots movements. Unlike hierarchical organizations, decentralized movements are harder to dismantle because they do not rely on a single leader or centralized structure. They empower individuals at every level to take ownership of the struggle, making them more adaptable and resilient in the face of opposition.

Technology plays a critical role in enabling decentralization. Digital platforms allow grassroots organizers to coordinate efforts, share resources, and amplify their voices without the need for traditional institutions. Crowdfunding platforms provide financial support, social media spreads awareness, and encrypted messaging apps ensure secure communication. These tools make it possible for grassroots movements to operate on a global scale while remaining rooted in local communities.

Connecting Local Struggles to Global Movements

One of the challenges grassroots movements face is overcoming the sense of isolation that can arise when fighting systemic injustices. The Rising TIDE strategy emphasizes the importance of connecting local struggles to larger, global movements. This not only provides a sense of solidarity but also amplifies the impact of each individual effort.

For example, indigenous land defenders fighting resource extraction in one region can connect with similar movements in other parts of the world, sharing strategies and building networks of support. Environmental activists addressing climate change can collaborate across borders, creating a unified front against the fossil fuel industry. By framing local issues as part of a global fight against systemic greed and corruption, grassroots movements can inspire collective action that transcends geographic and cultural boundaries.

Inspiring Action Through Storytelling

Storytelling is a powerful tool for inspiring action and building solidarity. Grassroots movements thrive on the ability to connect individual experiences to broader systemic issues, making the abstract tangible and the distant personal. Stories of resistance, resilience, and triumph remind people that change is possible and that they are not alone in their struggles.

The Rising TIDE strategy encourages grassroots organizers to use storytelling to build empathy and inspire action. By highlighting the human impact of systemic greed, whether it's families displaced by resource extraction, workers exploited by corporations, or communities devastated by climate change, movements can galvanize public support and motivate people to join the fight.

Empowering Communities to Act

Empowerment is the final piece of the Rising TIDE strategy. It's not enough to inspire people, they must also have the tools and resources to take action. This means providing training, sharing knowledge, and building networks that enable communities to organize effectively. It also means creating spaces where people feel safe to voice their concerns, share their ideas, and take ownership of their collective future.

Grassroots movements must prioritize inclusivity, ensuring that marginalized voices are heard and represented. This includes addressing systemic barriers that prevent participation, such as lack of access to technology or resources. By building inclusive movements, the Rising TIDE strategy ensures that the fight against systemic greed is truly representative of the people it seeks to empower.

Moving Forward Together

The power of grassroots movements lies in their ability to inspire and empower people to act collectively. They remind us that we don't need permission from politicians or corporations to demand justice, we already have the power to create change. The Rising TIDE strategy is a call to action for communities to rise together, leveraging their collective strength to dismantle the systems of greed and corruption that have held them back for too long.

By inspiring and empowering grassroots movements, we can create a world where power is decentralized, accountability is the norm, and equity is a reality. This is not just a vision for the future, it's a roadmap for action today. The Rising TIDE is rising, and it begins with us.

~14
The Technology of Opposition

Harnessing AI, Blockchain, and Smart Contracts

Technology has long been a double-edged sword, capable of both liberating humanity and reinforcing oppressive systems. In the fight against fascism and systemic greed, the key lies in harnessing technology as a tool for disruption, transparency, and accountability. The power of technologies like artificial intelligence (AI), blockchain, and smart contracts lies in their ability to bypass corrupt intermediaries and create systems that prioritize fairness, decentralization, and equity over profit and control.

Disrupting Fascist Systems with Technology

Fascist systems thrive on control, control of information, resources, and people. Technology offers an unprecedented opportunity to disrupt these systems by decentralizing power and empowering individuals. At its core, the use of AI, blockchain, and smart contracts can dismantle the mechanisms of greed and corruption that underpin authoritarian regimes and exploitative corporations. These tools are not merely tools of resistance; they are instruments of systemic reinvention, capable of creating new paradigms of governance, finance, and law.

For example, AI has the potential to process vast amounts of data to uncover corruption, identify systemic inefficiencies, and hold those in power accountable. By using machine learning algorithms to analyze financial transactions, contracts, and public records, AI can expose patterns of fraud, tax evasion, and abuse of power that would otherwise remain hidden. However, this potential must be balanced with safeguards to prevent AI from being co-opted by the same systems it seeks to dismantle. Left unchecked, AI can just as easily be weaponized to surveil and control as it can to liberate.

Blockchain technology, on the other hand, offers a decentralized alternative to traditional systems of governance and finance. By creating immutable, transparent records, blockchain eliminates the need for centralized authorities that can be corrupted or manipulated. In governance, blockchain can be used to ensure fair and transparent elections, free from tampering or fraud. In finance, it can facilitate peer-to-peer transactions that bypass banks and financial institutions, reducing the influence of corporate greed. Blockchain's potential to disrupt oppressive systems is immense, but its implementation must be guided by principles of equity and accessibility to avoid replicating existing hierarchies.

Smart contracts, powered by blockchain, further extend this potential by automating processes and ensuring compliance without the need for intermediaries. These self-executing contracts are governed by code, not by human discretion, making them less vulnerable to corruption. For example, smart contracts can be used to distribute aid directly to those in need, bypassing bureaucracies and ensuring that resources reach their intended recipients. They can also enforce accountability in business and governance, automatically penalizing noncompliance with agreed-upon terms. By removing the human element, smart contracts reduce the risk of exploitation and ensure fairness in transactions.

Replacing Corrupt Intermediaries

The true power of these technologies lies in their ability to replace the corrupt intermediaries that dominate current systems. In governance, this means creating decentralized models where decision-making is transparent and participatory, rather than controlled by elites. Imagine a system where laws and budgets are determined not by self-serving politicians but by a collective vote on a secure blockchain platform, accessible to anyone with a smartphone. This is not a utopian fantasy, it is a practical application of existing technology.

In finance, blockchain and smart contracts can disrupt the monopoly of banks and financial institutions, which have long exploited the most vulnerable through predatory lending, excessive fees, and discriminatory practices. Decentralized finance (DeFi) platforms already demonstrate how individuals can access financial services without relying on traditional banks. By prioritizing transparency and inclusivity, these platforms can democratize access to resources and reduce economic inequality.

Similarly, in law, smart contracts have the potential to create a more equitable legal system by automating compliance and ensuring that agreements are enforced impartially. This eliminates the need for costly legal battles and reduces the influence of wealth and privilege in determining outcomes. These technologies offer a glimpse into a future where systems of power are designed to serve the many, not the few.

Designing Tech Immune to the "Greed Virus"

While the potential of these technologies is immense, their success depends on how they are designed and implemented. The "greed virus," the insatiable pursuit of profit at any cost, has already corrupted many aspects of technology, from surveillance capitalism to the proliferation of exploitative financial products. To avoid replicating these patterns, it is essential to design systems that are immune to human intervention and manipulation.

This begins with decentralization. By removing centralized points of control, blockchain and AI systems become less susceptible to corruption and abuse. Decentralized governance models, for instance, distribute decision-making power across a network, ensuring that no single entity can dominate. Similarly, open-source development allows for greater transparency and accountability, as anyone can audit the code and contribute to its improvement.

Ethical design is another critical component. Technologies must be built with principles of equity, accessibility, and sustainability at their core. This means prioritizing the needs of marginalized communities, ensuring that tools are user-friendly and inclusive, and minimizing environmental impact. It also means rejecting business models that rely on surveillance, exploitation, or profit maximization at the expense of human dignity.

Education is key to achieving these goals. Technologists and innovators must be equipped with the knowledge and skills to build systems that align with these principles. This requires a cultural shift within the tech industry, moving away from a focus on profit and toward a commitment to social good. Young innovators, in particular, have the potential to lead this shift, bringing fresh perspectives and bold ideas to the table.

Encouraging Innovators to Prioritize Equity

The future of technology depends on the choices we make today. Encouraging technologists and young innovators to prioritize decentralized, equitable systems over profit-driven models is essential to realizing the full potential of AI, blockchain, and smart contracts. This requires creating spaces where innovation can thrive without the influence of corporate greed or government control.

Hackathons, incubators, and open-source communities provide opportunities for collaboration and experimentation, allowing innovators to develop solutions that address real-world problems. These spaces must be inclusive, welcoming diverse voices and perspectives that reflect the needs of the broader community. By fostering a culture of innovation rooted in equity and accountability, we can ensure that technology serves as a force for liberation rather than oppression.

At the same time, it is important to recognize that technology alone cannot solve systemic issues. While AI, blockchain, and smart contracts are powerful tools, they must be part of a larger strategy that includes grassroots organizing, policy advocacy, and cultural change. Technology is not a silver bullet, but it can amplify and accelerate efforts to create a more just and equitable world.

The Path Forward

Harnessing technology to disrupt fascist systems and replace corrupt intermediaries is both a challenge and an opportunity. The Rising TIDE strategy provides a framework for leveraging these tools to create systems that prioritize transparency, accountability, and equity. By embracing decentralization, ethical design, and inclusive innovation, we can build a future where technology empowers the many rather than enriching the few.

This is not just a fight against fascism, it is a fight for the soul of technology itself. Will it be used to reinforce greed and oppression, or will it become a force for liberation and justice? The choice is ours to make, and the stakes could not be higher. The time to act is now, and the tools are already in our hands. The Rising TIDE is rising, are we ready to rise with it?

Case Studies in Tech-Driven Opposition

Technology has already proven its potential to disrupt oppressive systems and empower movements for justice. Across the globe, innovators and activists are leveraging tools like blockchain, AI, and open-source platforms to combat authoritarianism, challenge corporate greed, and amplify grassroots opposition. These case studies demonstrate that the tools for systemic change are not only possible, they are already in use.

Blockchain for Transparency and Accountability

In countries plagued by corruption and authoritarian control, blockchain technology is being used to ensure transparency in governance. For example, during elections, blockchain has been piloted as a tool to create tamper-proof voting records. By recording votes on an immutable ledger, blockchain eliminates the possibility of election fraud and ensures that results are transparent and verifiable. In places like Sierra Leone, blockchain-based voting trials have shown the potential for restoring trust in electoral systems that are often manipulated by the ruling elite.

Beyond elections, blockchain is also being used to track the flow of government funds. In regions where public money is routinely siphoned off by corrupt officials, blockchain provides an unalterable record of transactions, making it harder for funds to disappear without accountability. This technology has been applied in anti-corruption initiatives, where governments and NGOs use it to ensure that aid reaches its intended recipients without being intercepted by intermediaries.

Blockchain's decentralized nature makes it especially powerful in regions where centralized authorities cannot be trusted. By removing the need for gatekeepers, blockchain empowers citizens to demand accountability and transparency, breaking the cycle of corruption that underpins many authoritarian regimes.

Decentralized Fundraising for Grassroots Movements

Crowdfunding platforms, often powered by blockchain, have become a vital tool for grassroots movements. In authoritarian states where traditional fundraising channels are blocked or monitored, decentralized platforms provide a way for activists to gather resources securely and anonymously. For example, during the protests in Belarus against Alexander Lukashenko's regime, activists used decentralized platforms to raise funds for legal aid, medical supplies, and organizing efforts.

By bypassing traditional financial systems, decentralized fundraising allows movements to sustain themselves without reliance on compromised institutions. These platforms also democratize access to funding, enabling ordinary people to contribute directly to causes they believe in. This financial independence is crucial for movements operating in hostile environments, where reliance on external institutions can leave them vulnerable to shutdowns or crackdowns.

AI for Exposing Disinformation

The rise of authoritarian regimes and fascist systems has been fueled in part by the spread of disinformation. Social media platforms, driven by profit and engagement metrics, have amplified false narratives and conspiracy theories, undermining trust in democratic institutions and sowing division. However, AI is now being used to combat this disinformation, exposing the tactics used by bad actors to manipulate public discourse.

For example, AI-driven tools can analyze patterns of activity on social media to identify bot networks and coordinated disinformation campaigns. These tools have been used to expose state-sponsored propaganda efforts, such as those linked to Russia's interference in foreign elections or China's promotion of its authoritarian policies abroad. By revealing the sources and methods of disinformation, AI empowers citizens and journalists to hold these regimes accountable and counteract their narratives.

AI is also being used to fact-check information in real time. Platforms like Logically and Factmata use machine learning algorithms to verify the accuracy of news articles and social media posts, providing users with reliable information and countering the spread of falsehoods. These tools are not only defensive, they are offensive measures in the fight against authoritarianism, reclaiming public discourse from those who seek to distort it.

Open-Source Platforms for Organizing and Collaboration

Grassroots movements around the world are increasingly turning to open-source platforms to organize and collaborate without reliance on traditional gatekeepers. These platforms provide activists with secure, decentralized tools for communication, coordination, and resource sharing. For example, encrypted messaging apps like Signal and Matrix have become indispensable for protest organizers, enabling them to plan actions and share information without fear of surveillance.

Open-source platforms also allow for the creation of collaborative tools that can be adapted to the specific needs of a movement. For instance, during the Hong Kong protests, activists developed decentralized apps to track police movements, share protest locations, and coordinate logistics.

These tools, created and maintained by the community, demonstrate the power of open-source collaboration in empowering grassroots efforts.

In addition to logistical support, open-source platforms foster the exchange of ideas and strategies between movements. Activists can share best practices, learn from each other's successes and failures, and build networks of solidarity across borders. This global exchange strengthens the collective fight against authoritarianism and systemic greed, showing that the struggle is not isolated but interconnected.

Creative Resistance Through Technology

Technology has also enabled new forms of creative resistance that challenge authoritarian regimes and corporate greed in innovative ways. Digital art, for example, has become a powerful tool for raising awareness and inspiring action. Artists use blockchain to create and distribute works that highlight social injustices, with the proceeds often going directly to support grassroots movements.

Similarly, activists have used social media to stage digital protests, flooding platforms with messages of dissent and disrupting the narratives promoted by authoritarian regimes. During the Black Lives Matter protests, hashtags like #BlackLivesMatter and #EndSARS in Nigeria became rallying points for global solidarity, amplifying the voices of those on the frontlines and putting pressure on governments to act.

Creative resistance also includes the use of technology to subvert systems of control. Hacktivist groups like Anonymous have targeted authoritarian governments and corporations, exposing secrets, disrupting operations, and demonstrating the vulnerabilities of those who claim absolute power. These acts of digital dissent remind us that no system is invincible and

that technology can be a weapon for justice as well as
oppression.

Challenges and Opportunities Ahead

While these case studies show the potential of technology to
disrupt fascist systems and empower opposition movements,
they also highlight the challenges that lie ahead. Authoritarian
regimes and corporations are not passive actors, they are
actively working to co-opt and neutralize these tools. From
surveillance technologies to algorithmic biases, the same
innovations that empower movements can also be weaponized
against them.

To navigate this landscape, it is essential to remain vigilant
and adaptive. Grassroots movements and technologists must
prioritize ethical design, transparency, and inclusivity in their
work, ensuring that the tools they create serve the many rather
than the few. Collaboration between activists, technologists,
and communities is key to staying ahead of those who seek to
maintain the status quo.

A Vision for Tech-Driven Opposition

The power of technology lies not in its ability to resist but in its
capacity to reinvent. These case studies show that technology
can do more than disrupt oppressive systems, it can replace
them with alternatives that are transparent, decentralized, and
equitable. By building on these successes and addressing the
challenges, we can create a future where technology serves as a
force for liberation rather than oppression.

The Rising TIDE strategy calls on all of us, technologists,
activists, and citizens alike, to embrace the possibilities of tech-
driven opposition. The tools for change are already in our

hands. It is now up to us to use them to dismantle the systems of greed and build a world where equity, justice, and sustainability are not just ideals but realities. The tide is rising, and with it comes the opportunity to shape a better future.

Special Note: Remember Who They Are

The billionaires, oligarchs, and corporate elites who dominate our world are not role models, they are rich, evil sociopaths driven by greed and devoid of humanity. Aspiring to their wealth is aspiring to their emptiness. Their power comes not from brilliance or innovation but from exploitation and systemic manipulation. We don't need to emulate their sociopathy; we need to reject it entirely.

Instead, we must prioritize new, or perhaps ancient, ways of valuing each other. Compassion, community, equity, and care are the real markers of a thriving society. Let's redefine success as the ability to uplift one another, not to hoard wealth at the expense of others. A better world starts with valuing humanity over profit.

~15
The Rising TIDE Era

Replacing Corrupt Systems with Decentralized Governance

The world's current power structures, dominated by greed, corruption, and incompetence, are not only failing humanity but actively endangering our future. From authoritarian governments to corporate oligarchies, these centralized systems are outdated relics of a past built on exploitation and control. It is time to replace them with decentralized governance systems that prioritize equity, transparency, and collective well-being. With the tools of today, smartphones, blockchain, and AI-driven solutions, this transformation is not only possible but urgently necessary.

Decentralized governance offers a radical alternative to the systems that have betrayed us. Imagine a world where decisions about laws, budgets, and community priorities are not made in backrooms by elites but are determined collectively by the people they impact. With digital tools like blockchain, individuals can participate directly in governance through secure and transparent voting systems. These tools eliminate the need for corrupt intermediaries, ensuring that every voice is heard and every decision is accounted for. Smart contracts can automate the enforcement of collective agreements, reducing opportunities for manipulation and corruption. This is not a distant dream, it is an achievable reality if we are willing to embrace the possibilities of technology.

The key to decentralized governance lies in the accessibility of modern tools. Nearly everyone has access to a cell phone, which can serve as a gateway to participatory governance. Through secure apps and platforms, citizens can vote on policies, allocate budgets, and propose solutions to community challenges. These tools empower individuals to take control of

their futures without relying on politicians who have
repeatedly proven their loyalty to corporate donors over their
constituents. By cutting out these intermediaries, decentralized
systems return power to where it belongs: in the hands of the
people.

The current power structures have rendered themselves
obsolete. Their greed, incompetence, and short-sightedness
have created a world on the brink of environmental collapse,
economic inequality, and widespread disillusionment. These
systems are not just broken, they are actively harmful. The
individuals who perpetuate them, from corporate CEOs to
political leaders, have shown time and time again that they are
incapable of prioritizing humanity's collective good. They
have hoarded wealth, eroded trust, and dismantled the very
institutions designed to protect us. They are not fit to govern,
and it is time to replace them with systems that can.

The dismantling of public education is one of the most
egregious examples of how current systems have failed. By
systematically underfunding schools, devaluing teachers, and
prioritizing profits over knowledge, these systems have created
a compliant, uninformed populace that is easier to control.
Education should be the foundation of a thriving society,
equipping individuals with the tools to think critically,
challenge authority, and participate meaningfully in
governance. Instead, it has been weaponized to maintain the
status quo, leaving generations ill-prepared to confront the
challenges of the modern world.

Decentralized governance calls for a new standard of
education, one that prioritizes empowerment over compliance.
With access to digital tools and global knowledge networks,
individuals can bypass traditional gatekeepers of information
and take control of their own learning. Online courses, open-
source materials, and community-driven education initiatives
can equip people with the skills they need to govern
themselves and hold systems accountable. By decentralizing

education alongside governance, we can create a society that values knowledge, critical thinking, and collective action over obedience and ignorance.

Replacing corrupt systems with decentralized governance is not just an opportunity; it is a necessity. The tools are already in our hands, and the failures of the current systems are impossible to ignore. This is the moment to embrace a new world order, one that prioritizes humanity, equity, and sustainability over greed, control, and exploitation. Decentralized governance offers a vision for the future that is both practical and transformative, showing us that the power to govern ourselves has always been ours to claim.

Collective Action and the Inevitability of Change

The inevitability of replacing corrupt systems lies not just in their failures but in the growing power of collective action. Across the world, people are waking up to the fact that these systems, whether political, economic, or educational, exist to serve the few at the expense of the many. The façade of legitimacy that once shielded them is crumbling, revealing the greed, incompetence, and exploitation at their core. Decentralized governance is not just an ideal solution; it is the natural evolution of a society that refuses to be controlled by outdated hierarchies.

The fight is no longer about left versus right, it is about up versus down. It is the people versus those who have hoarded power and wealth, exploiting our labor, our resources, and our planet. This isn't a battle between political parties; it's a fundamental conflict between systems that perpetuate oppression and the collective force of humanity demanding liberation. Decentralized governance represents the ultimate tool for reclaiming that power. It allows us to bypass the structures that have failed us and create systems that are truly of, by, and for the people.

Collective action is the engine driving this transformation. It begins with individuals recognizing their shared struggles and connecting their efforts across borders, industries, and communities. Movements that once fought separately, whether for climate justice, racial equality, or economic reform, are now uniting under the shared understanding that their battles are deeply interconnected. The tools of decentralization amplify this collective power, providing platforms for collaboration, communication, and action on an unprecedented scale.

Imagine a global network of decentralized movements working together to dismantle the systems of greed. Environmental activists in the Amazon could coordinate directly with technologists in Silicon Valley, sharing resources and strategies to combat deforestation and corporate exploitation. Workers in underpaid industries could use blockchain platforms to demand transparency in supply chains, holding corporations accountable for their practices. Educators could collaborate on open-source curricula that prioritize critical thinking and civic engagement, equipping future generations to govern themselves. The possibilities are limitless when collective action is paired with the tools of decentralization.

At the heart of this vision is the understanding that the current systems cannot be fixed, they must be replaced. Voting harder, begging elected officials to act, or hoping for incremental change will not address the scale of the crises we face. These systems were designed to serve the interests of the wealthy and powerful, and they will not willingly relinquish their control. Decentralized governance offers a way to bypass their stranglehold entirely, creating a new paradigm that prioritizes humanity over profit.

This isn't resistance; it's reinvention. Resistance implies fighting within the parameters of the existing system, while reinvention involves creating something entirely new.

156

Decentralized governance rejects the idea that we must work within the confines of corruption and greed. Instead, it offers a vision for a future where power is distributed, accountability is non-negotiable, and decision-making is truly democratic. It is a rejection of everything the current systems represent and a declaration that we will not accept their limitations.

The inevitability of change is not just a hopeful idea, it is a historical truth. Every empire, every oppressive regime, every corrupt institution has eventually fallen under the weight of its own failures. What replaces them, however, depends on the actions of those who rise to meet the moment. Decentralized governance ensures that the systems we build next are not just replacements but improvements, designed to serve humanity rather than control it.

This is a call to action for everyone, technologists, educators, activists, and everyday citizens. The tools for change are already in our hands, but tools alone are not enough. It takes collective will and determination to wield them effectively. It takes the courage to reject what no longer works and the imagination to build what will. It takes the belief that we, the many, have the power to reclaim our future from the greedy, incompetent few who have failed us.

The current systems are collapsing under their own weight, but it is up to us to decide what comes next. Decentralized governance is not just a solution, it is a promise. A promise that power can be returned to the people, that equity can replace exploitation, and that justice can prevail over greed. This isn't the end of the story; it's the beginning of something new. The tide is turning, and with it comes the opportunity to shape a world that works for everyone, not just the privileged few. The time to act is now, and the power to do so has always been ours. Together, we can replace, rebuild, and repeat, until justice, equity, and humanity prevail.

Epilogue

Stop Begging the System to Fix Itself

The time for asking, pleading, and waiting is over. The system we live under is not broken, it is working exactly as it was designed to: to consolidate power and wealth in the hands of the few while exploiting the many. Local "electeds," national politicians, and even international leaders are not allies in this fight. They are the enablers of systemic greed, placed in positions of authority not to serve the people, but to protect the interests of their donors, lobbyists, and corporate backers. Begging these individuals to act, writing letters, attending town halls, or hoping for change from within the system only perpetuates the illusion of democracy while allowing the real oppressors to continue their exploitation unchecked.

Instead of directing energy toward these hollow institutions, we must focus on the real architects of oppression: the corporations and billionaires who have bought and corrupted governments worldwide. Begin local, regional, and national protests, not outside the offices of politicians but directly targeting the headquarters, events, and infrastructure of the corporate oppressors themselves. Public demonstrations, boycotts, and divestment campaigns must center on the industries and individuals who fuel the greed virus, sending a clear message that their unchecked power will no longer be tolerated.

This complacency and misplaced trust in "electeds" is not accidental. It is the result of decades of systematic dismantling of public education, designed to produce a compliant, uninformed populace that lacks the critical thinking skills to recognize or challenge the systems of oppression around them. Ignorance is not a coincidence; it is a deliberate strategy to maintain control. A populace that is kept in the dark, through defunded schools, manipulated curriculums, and propaganda masquerading as media, is far easier to control. And yet, two things can be true at once: many voters are victims of this system, manipulated into compliance, but they are still responsible for their actions. Just as an abuser cannot excuse their behavior by citing past trauma, voters who perpetuate oppression through their choices must be held accountable while also acknowledging the systemic forces that shaped their beliefs.

But accountability is not about blame, it is about change. Acknowledging the failures of the current system and its enablers allows us to move forward with clarity. The tools for bypassing these corrupt systems are already in our hands. Technology, when wielded with purpose and responsibility, empowers us to govern ourselves, to create systems that are transparent, equitable, and decentralized. Blockchain, smart contracts, and AI-driven governance are not just abstract solutions, they are practical tools that can replace the broken systems of today with something far better.

The conclusion is simple: stop relying on the system to fix itself. It won't. The time for begging and hoping is over. The time for action, reinvention, and reclamation has arrived.

Reinvention and the Call to Action

If there's one lesson we must take to heart, it's that the current systems are incapable of reform. They were designed to serve the interests of the elite, not the people. Their failures are not bugs but features, intentional outcomes of a structure built to perpetuate inequality, greed, and control. It's not enough to resist these systems. Resistance implies working within their framework, patching their cracks, and hoping they'll work for us someday. But these systems cannot work for us. They must be replaced, entirely and permanently.

160

The tools to replace them are already here. Technology has evolved to the point where it can empower us to reclaim governance, rewrite priorities, and dismantle corruption. Blockchain and smart contracts offer transparency and accountability that traditional governments have failed to deliver. AI can analyze vast data sets, identify inefficiencies, and create equitable resource allocations. With these tools, we can govern ourselves, setting laws, budgets, and priorities collectively, bypassing the corrupt intermediaries that have held power for too long.

This is the ultimate act of reinvention: using the same tools that the powerful have wielded against us to rebuild systems that work for everyone. If they have automated and outsourced humanity for their profit, we will automate and outsource them for our survival. This is not revenge; it is necessity. Their incompetence, greed, and sociopathy have disqualified them from power. It is time for the many to reclaim what the few have stolen: the ability to determine our collective future.

This reinvention requires a shift in how we think about power and governance. No longer should we accept the idea that politicians or corporations will save us. The cavalry isn't coming, we are the cavalry. Real change will come from collective action, grassroots organizing, and the intentional use of technology to create systems that prioritize equity over profit, transparency over secrecy, and humanity over greed.

The challenge before us is immense, but so is our capacity for transformation. We've seen it in movements across history, where people have risen up against oppression and rebuilt systems to serve the greater good. This moment is no different. It demands that we come together, that we reject division and distraction, and that we focus on what truly matters: reclaiming power, rebuilding systems, and ensuring justice for all.

Let this be a rallying cry. If they say we can't govern ourselves, prove them wrong. If they say the system is too big to fail, prove them wrong. If they say resistance is futile, prove them wrong by refusing to resist and instead reinvent. The power to replace, rebuild, and repeat is already in our hands. Together, we can create a world where equity, justice, and humanity are not aspirations but realities. The time to act is now. Let's begin.

Final Note: The Mask Is Off

I know you don't want to hear this, and I wish it weren't true, but maybe this is a good thing. Maybe the collapse of the illusion, the pretense that this was ever a functioning democracy, that meritocracy wasn't a lie, that fairness existed, is the first step toward something better. The mask is off, and we see the truth: this is an oligarchy, half the population is in a cult, and the rest of us are holding on by a thread. You are not crazy. We are all suffering from trauma, from collective PTSD, from the relentless grind of living in a world where greed and corruption run unchecked. And yet, here we are. We go on. Because it's the right thing to do.

The truth is, this pain, this chaos, this rawness, it's clarifying. It reminds us what matters. The people around us, the communities we build, the art we create, the moments of joy we carve out even in the darkest times. Use the tools at your disposal. Lean on each other. Make art. Scream into the void. Get mad. Get happy. Laugh. Dance. Love. Do not let these freaks and sickos grind you into despair. They thrive on fear, on apathy, on your belief that you're powerless. Prove them wrong every single day.

Fight. Fight for your future, for your neighbor, for the planet, for yourself. Fight with your mind, your heart, your voice, your actions. Fight until they can't take one more inch from you. And when you're tired, rest, but never surrender. This is our time, our moment to say, "No more." We didn't choose this battle, but we will win it. Because we must. Because there's no other choice. And because we are many, and they are few.

and the winner is…

Tech and the techno-feudalists, of course. The ones who promised us liberation, efficiency, and connection but instead built gilded cages disguised as progress. In the world of comics, the villain's motives are always painfully clear, they crave power for its own sake, to dominate and destroy because they can. In 2025, our villains wear hoodies, wield algorithms, and call themselves disruptors. They didn't just disrupt industries; they disrupted democracy, truth, and humanity itself.

Look around: the billionaire class, our so-called techno-feudalists, has taken the tools that could have lifted humanity to new heights and twisted them into weapons of control. They didn't automate for equality; they automated for profit. They didn't connect the world; they isolated us into echo chambers and sold us lies. They didn't create to empower; they created to enslave. All the while, they told us it was inevitable, that this was just the cost of innovation.

It didn't have to be this way. Technology could have been the great equalizer, the tool to dismantle oppression, and the key to human freedom. But in the hands of techno-feudalists, it became a digital empire, a playground for billionaires and a dystopia for everyone else. So yes, in the story of fascism and greed, the winner, for now, is tech. Not because technology is inherently evil but because those wielding it have chosen domination over decency, profit over people, and greed over the greater good. But like every comic villain, their power is their undoing. Because if they can use technology for evil, we can use it for good. They've built the tools; now it's up to us to take them back, to rewrite the ending, and to ensure that this time, the hero wins. Fair is fair.

About EATMS Productions

What's happening to women now is not random. It's structural.

Policy, culture, technology, and power are moving in the same direction.

EATMS maps them clearly and shows how to respond.

This title is part of an ongoing body of work. All EATMS Productions titles, across all series, authors, and formats, are components of a single connected project.

Start here: EATMS System Primer — Free Bundle
https://eatms.gumroad.com/l/dyvzbw

For full catalog or inquiries: eatms.me

Free survival booklet + EATMS updates: email "EATMS" to eatms@pm.me

Please feel free to burn part or all of this book, safely, as an effigy.